The Yi Jing Apocrypha
of
Genghis Khan

Black Dragon Society's Treatise on the Art of Ninzuwu

Edited and translated

by

Warlock Asylum

The Yi Jing Apocrypha of Genghis Khan

ISBN: 1492750859
ISBN-13: 978-1492750857

The Yi Jing Apocrypha of Genghis Khan

"I had no place to hide from thunder, so, I am not afraid of it anymore... With Heaven's aid, I have conquered for you a huge empire. But my life was too short to achieve the conquest of the world. That task is left for you."- Genghis Khan

TABLE OF CONTENTS

The Language of Ninzuwu

A = 🝆 = ah   B = 🝆 = bee   C = 🝆 = xek

D = 🝆 = duh   E = 🝆 = eh   F = 🝆 = f

G = 🝆 = gi   H = 🝆 = whoo

I = 🝆 = ee   J = 🝆 = jo   K = 🝆 = kuh

L = 🝆 = le   M = 🝆 = mmh   N = 🝆 = nn

O = 🝆 = oh   P = 🝆 = ph   Q = 🝆 = ach

R = 🝆 = ru   S = 🝆 = hss   T = 🝆 = te

U = 🝆 = yu   V = 🝆 = veh   W = 🝆 = wu

X = 🝆 = ie   Y = 🝆 = ui   Z = 🝆 = zz

THE VASUH SCRIPT

ZHEE   AUM   TUU

HMU   BNHU   PHE

NZU   LEWHU   SHKI

The Yi Jing Apocrypha of Genghis Khan

+

Introduction

My initiation into the Art of Ninzuwu (Yi Jing sorcery) began over 14 years ago. It was a very intense time in my life as I was forced to deal with some of life's challenges. I took faith, however, in writing poetry as a means of salvation and for healing old wounds. One day, while attending a poetry venue that I would often frequent, a friend of mine saw me reading the I Ching and invited me over to her house to discuss a few things. I had recently bought a copy of the book from a used thrift shop and was curious about its wisdom and application.

When I arrived at my friend's home, she revealed another side of herself that I knew nothing about. We would meet about once a week thereafter. What she told me about the world would change my life forever.

I was fascinated by the wisdom of this woman and was curious about the origins of such knowledge. She would often reply in a calm voice, saying: "Oh, you can find this knowledge in any religion." I didn't understand what she meant at the time, but today her words are very clear to me. Your spiritual path is simply the tools you use to adapt to life's changes, nothing more and nothing less. There is, however, a technology that can be used to navigate through the world's current much more effectively after understanding what the "world" really is. This technology is known by many names, but popularly, as magic and occultism.

Unfortunately, the time with my new-found mentor was brief. She was of a class of magicians who knew how to prepare for her next life by obtaining a human vessel that could be used as a vehicle and projecting herself into its psyche, a form of technology that was practiced by ancient Taoist adepts. My mentor told me that when she met her teacher, it was while reading the I Ching. Her teacher told her that he would return to her as a man in his late-twenties with a Middle Eastern name.

After my mentor transpired into the invisible realms, the knowledge she taught me weighed heavily on my mind. I was raised in a Christian home and was accustom to seeing things from a religious perspective. This too was soon to change as I began to study the occult, even associating myself with certain known magical organizations in my area. What I began to notice is that many people who call themselves magicians are just as blind as the religious people they laugh at. In many cases, the only difference between the religious and magical community, is that one group is working with a religious form that is slightly older than the other, but call it magic. It still comes down to executing some of the same practices used in the Abrahamic religious circle that these same magicians often ridicule. To say that there isn't any hierarchy in the scheme of life is foolish. We see our civilization is setup and regulated by authority. Authority isn't the issue here, but our means to be able to evolve spiritually is. It was then that I sought initiation.

I came to understand many things in my studies, and among these was the value of initiation. This came to me during my early meetings with an Ifa Priest. He would provide me with spiritual cleanings. During my wait time at his office, we would talk about some of his clients, their issues and how they were resolved. It was very fascinating to hear such stories and I began to see how experiences can be created and ended by the magician. Some of the stories were a bit dark for my taste, but one thing he did emphasize was the value of initiation. He told me how some workers of the "dark arts" even had the ability to take someone else's life and how many of the crimes that occur in the world today are a result of evil magic. The only problem for me at that time was the cost of initiation. Initiation into Ifa may cost the candidate thousands of dollars and I didn't have that type of money to spend. I was, however, initiated into Reiki, which focused more on healing while helping me understand some things about Eastern philosophy.

About two years passed, I was in a bookstore, just looking to see if there were any interesting titles in the New Age section, and came across the Simon Necronomicon. It was an interesting book. But after arriving home and doing some research about the tome, I decided not to pursue using this book, as it was deemed to be a "hoax."

My curiosity in the Simon tome still persisted. Over the next few years, I spent a lot of time studying Sumerian mythology. This was mainly due to the thesis, as many scholars still hold, that Sumeria was the world's first civilization. I knew the history of the Abrahamic religions, but wasn't attracted to any of these perspectives. If I was going to become a magician it would involve a form of magic that didn't have even the slightest hint of Biblical dogma. So I decided to obtain a copy of the Simon Necronomicon Spellbook and work with the Fifty Names of Marduk. My experiments with the Fifty Names of Marduk went extremely well. My interest in the Simon tome was rekindled. I must remind the reader at this point that while there is much debate about the "Necronomicon," users of the Simon tome don't believe in Lovecraft's idea of a "Necronomicon." The use of the term here has much to do with a Sumerian grimoire with the same title. Hopefully, this should settle some confusion in this regard.

Shortly after experimenting with the Necronomicon Spellbook, I came into contact with someone who knew how to walk the initiatory gates listed in the Simon tome. It wouldn't cost me thousands of dollars. Instead, what I couldn't afford in currency, I would pay for in time and study. The initiation was very transformational to say the least. I gained more knowledge about the DinGir (Sumerian gods) than many who were educated in such studies. The workings of the tome were confirmed by friends and associates who practiced African Divination. It wasn't that they were familiar with the Simon tome, but was confirmed in that the same practices and structure of the Simon tome were also exercised in Ifa. This was very encouraging in the wake of all the negative propaganda that the book had received. In further interest of increasing my knowledge about the tome, I started the Papers in the Attic blog page. It began as a sort of personal journal. The title was a rebuttal to Dan Harms' blog called Papers Falling from an Attic Window, which focused more on debunking Simon's tome. Dan and I were in heavy debate at the time, but today we enjoy a good friendship.

While the joy over my initiation continued, I still had some concerns about the practice. My mentor used to always emphasize the need to test and validate information. This was the motto of an occult organization I joined a few years prior to my initiation. There were also discrepancies that I discovered in the idea that Sumer was the world's first civilization. Despite all of this, my initiation was a vital step along the path.

The objective behind my work began to change slightly. I wasn't as curious about the things that my first mentor had told my in regard to life and etc. At this point, I was completely absorbed in

Sumerian mysticism and in being a true son of
Ishtar. Suddenly, the idea came to me that I should
research an inclusive system, like Shinto, in order
to help me fill in some of the missing pieces that I
discovered in the Sumerian paradigm. My interest
in Shinto was inspired by a passage in the Voudon
Gnostic Workbook [1]about the spiritual system itself
and the Kami. After checking some resources
online, I discovered that the idea of someone of
non-Japanese descent being initiated into Shinto
was almost impossible. Of course, like every
practitioner of the Simon tome, this was even more
of a challenge that was worth overcoming. I
summoned my Watcher and two weeks later I was
invited to meet someone at an Esoteric Shinto
group called Worldmate. This was an amazing
experience and the people that I met there were
truly remarkable. What amazed me the most about
all of this is that many of their rituals and rites also
appeared in the ancient Mesopotamian paradigm.
It validated much of what is written in the Simon
tome. While there were some differences, the
knowledge I gained in Shinto helped me
understand the details I missed earlier concerning
the unseen world.

I began to differentiate between the worlds of black
and white magic with ease after my studies in

---

[1] The Voudon Gnostic Workbook by Michael Bertiaux (2007
Expanded edition) page 595: "The Kami, or the Gods of the Shinto
Religion, are the most powerful forces in the world. They are the
purest and most ideal embodiments of natural forces and elemental
power"

Shinto. I also discovered that magicians can be more religious than so-called religious people at times. Their experiences are filled with stories where a particular spirit told them about this and that. While many of these so-called magicians claim to see no value in "faith," they trust everything that a "spirit" tells them to do while their life is deteriorating. I do understand how such deception can occur as the magician is more sensitive to energy than the average human being. At times, this may mean that the magician is more impressionable than other human beings. They may follow a "hollow theory" long before the gullible when it's packaged right!

There is one rule which helped me greatly when working with Sumerian mysticism during this time. I made it a habit to always check the mythology of a said paradigm to see if the energy, or spirit, is running in accord with its equation. The right hemisphere of the brain is said to be the intuitive side, and interprets life in metaphor and symbol. The left hemisphere of the brain is said to be more logical and rational in thought. This means that even when explaining how intuitive energies operate, the ancients had to use mythology and symbols in their explanation. So if the magician has an encounter with an entity, they can always check and verify if this energy, or spirit, responds in the same fashion as its equation (mythology).

The other tool, which was a protection, as well as, an instrument of navigation, was my emotional state. In Eastern mysticism, an individual's emotional state determines if a spirit is a negative or positive form. Some energies are primal, and may cause one to feel uncomfortable due to such. But the majority of our experiences, while practicing divination should leave us feeling refreshed. In the case of primal energies, should give us a renewed faith to live life with virtue. Magical practices that require an unprecedented amount of exorcisms and banishings are just workings that invoke low-level spirits that deceive the practitioner, creating in them the belief that the "gods" need them to fulfill a special mission, very Christian indeed!

Another misconception that I began to observe during this time is the assumption that the magician needs to work with a force that can induce fatal consequences if necessary. While the editor of this text doesn't deny the truth of this in itself, this is not the goal of magical practice. Certainly, I witnessed and heard about such occurrences in my discussions with the Ifa Priest and others. However, psychic defense is countered primarily by virtue.

The physical realm is a direct reflection of the astral realm. One realm is not higher than the other, for they both rely on the divine world as its source of existence. However, in the phenomenal world we also find that there is a need for safety, but this need is more prevalent in areas that are infested with crime than not. Spiritually, we learn that those who are more concerned about working with a fatal force for protection, are those who are residing in an impoverished spiritual condition. This is evident by the fact that they are always in a state of disharmony and inspired to use magic for such purposes. What this means is that they have become consumed and convinced by low-level energies to engage in such conduct. In turn, the spirit, by the act of deception, will give them pseudo-occult power, but use their aura as a gate to cause havoc in their lives. They cannot see that the same spirits they invoke to help resolve a problem, are the same spirits causing the problem. These spirits are fed by constant invocation on the part of the practitioner, and when hungry, will create a situation where you feel the need to call on them. Christians, for example, feel a high level of protection from the Christ. Why aren't they overly concerned with using the Bible for such purposes? What I find interesting in all of this, is that people who do not know the value of virtue are the same people who are overly-concerned with these things. They are then influenced by emotions, spirits if you will, whose only concern is attacking other forms of humanity. Unfortunately, they made an error in thinking that intercourse with an evil force can lead to happiness.

During this time, something remarkable occurred. I was going through some old boxes, getting rid of some junk, and came across a box of books that belonged to my late mentor. Her neighbors gave me the books shortly after she left form. I had never seen these books before. There were a lot of Fourth Way writings and some works by Maurice Doreal, along with a version of the I Ching. I also found my mentor's journal in the box. This was very exciting discovery indeed. Finally, I wound be able to learn about the origin of the things that my mentor spoke to me about.

Something "miraculous" occurred after discovering her journal. In one section, she wrote about her dreams and experiences. Towards the rear of the journal, however, she left a list of things for me to do. This list perfectly described all of the spiritual arts and practices that I engaged in up until that point of finding her journal. I then learned of a secret society, similar to those described in Kenneth Gant's Cults of the Shadow, which held a special knowledge of the I Ching. It seemed that this Cult of Nyarzir and its practice of Ninzuwu originated in the East and advanced westward into what is known as ancient Sumeria. Proof of this will be discussed later in this introduction under the said topic.

Discovering this information was like a weight lifted off my shoulders, like the joy that a man experiences when he discovers his true heritage. Although my life was an open book to my friends and those around me, the knowledge about the Art of Ninzuwu I kept to myself. In some ways, it was for their own protection until I understood the true purpose of the art.

I would spend the next three years studying the Art of Ninzuwu, a system of I Ching Sorcery. During this time, my knowledge of ancient Sumeria grew at an astonishing rate. I began to take on students in the field of ancient Mesopotamian magic and spirituality. One of my first students was an Enochian magician named Rafael Barrio. My experiences in the field of Sumerian mysticism remained unprecedented and few knew that much of this phenomena had a lot to do with the Art of Ninzuwu.

Surprisingly, the Art of Ninzuwu didn't originate in ancient Mesopotamia, but in Asia. According to a certain history held by secret societies that practiced the Art of Ninzuwu. The Cult of Nyarzir began in the days of the legendary empire known as Mu. According to the history of Nyarzir, this was an empire that stretched from the Pacific Ocean and into the regions of what is known today as ancient Mesopotamia. Later, after the time of the deluge, the Empire of Mu fell and its residents divided themselves up into nations. It is also said in these oral traditions of the Ninzuwu that the Yi Jing was formulated during the time that this empire flourished.

My mentor was a third generation practitioner of the Art of Ninzuwu since its arrival here in America. Although the Cult of Nyarzir roots are said to stretch back to pre-Mesopotamian times, knowledge of the Art came to America by way of a Japanese man named Naka Nakane, who was a member of Japan's Black Dragon Society. Nakane constructed a time line, illustrating the history of how the teachings of the Cult of Nyarzir were preserved and some people of note who knew about the system. Unfortunately, my time with my mentor's journal was just as brief as our time before she left this plain of being. I was instructed to burn her journal and proceed to develop the art after the year 2012. The Art of Ninzuwu was never meant to be withheld from those less fortunate. On the contrary, it was developed in ancient times by those who sought the betterment of man.

Origin of the Yi Ching

The Yi Jing is the oldest of the Chinese classic texts. It is reported to be an ancient system of cosmology and philosophy, which inspired many Asian sciences. Traditionally, it is believed that the principles of the Yi Jing were discovered by Fu Xi, who is seen as a cultural hero and one of the earliest legendary rulers of China, approximately 2800 B.C.E. Legend has it that he received knowledge of the eight trigrams, the bagua, supernaturally.

Fu Xi is a very interesting figure indeed. His identity is important in determining the legacy of the Cult of Nyarzir. He is also said to be the inventor of writing, fishing and trapping. Another interesting factor about Fu Xi can be found in a Wikipedia article, under his name:

"According to legend, the land was swept by a great flood and only Fu Xi and his sister Nuwa survived. They retired to the mythological Kunlun Mountain, where they prayed for a sign from the Emperor of Heaven. The divine being

approved their union and the siblings set about procreating the human race."

The attributes recorded about Fu Xi are strikingly similar to the ancient Mesopotamian hero Ziusudra. Ziusudra, often labeled as the Sumerian Noah, was also a flood survivor. Amazingly, when the account of Fu Xi is compared to that of Ziusudra, we discover that Fu Xi is credited as having ruled around 2800 B.C.E. When we compare this with the WB-62 Sumerian King List, we find that Ziusudra is recorded to have inherited ruler-ship from his father Surrupak, who ruled for 10 sars. The next few lines read from the Sumerian King List read:

"Then the flood swept over. After the flood swept over, kingship descended from heaven; the kingship was in Kish."

Archeologists have attested to a river flood of proportional damage in Shurrupak and the surrounding Sumerian cities. According to the author Harriet Crawford, author of the work, *Sumer and the Sumerians,* this flood has been radiocarbon dated as having occurred around 2900 B.C.E. That's just a one-hundred year difference from the estimated time of Fu Xi's rule. Is it possible that Ziusudra and Fu Xi are the same person?

In the Gilgamesh Epics, Ziusudra is called Upnapishtim and the king of Shurrupak. He recounts to Gilgamesh how he survived the flood, sent by Enlil to wipe out humanity. Later, he is given the gift of immortality. Both the families of Fu Xi and Upnapishtim are said to be the sole deluge survivors in their perspective mythologies.

Another interesting aspect about the character Fu Xi is his description. Author Tao Huang, in the classic work, *Laoism: The Complete Teachings of Lao Zi*, states the following on page 232:

"In the case of Chinese history, when the Western Mother, who was a cosmic angel living on earth, gave birth to Fu Xi and Nu Wa, the brother and sister, they were all half human and half fish."

The description of Fu Xi and his wife, strikingly resembles the Seven Sages, the Apkallu, of ancient Mesopotamian lore. The Apkallu were said to have taught humanity the art of writing and other facets of civilization like Fu Xi. In the book, *Uriel's Machine* by Christopher Knight and Robert Lomas, we find that Fu Xi compares greatly to the Apkallu. Page 76 reads:

"So Utnapishtim, (or Ziusudra as he is also known) is the equivalent to the Biblical Noah. He was a king and priest of the Sumerian city of Shuruppak which is one of the original seven cities founded by the Seven Sages who the Sumerians believed were half man, half fish."

An often overlooked feature of the Apkallu is that in some mythologies they were credited with giving mankind the *"me."* The *"mes"* are the decrees of the gods and are often associated with the Tablets of Destinies. In the *Babylonian Myth of the Twenty-One Poultices*, we read:

"Nudimmud became angry and summoned the seven sages of Eridu in high tones, "Bring the document of my Anuship that it may be read before me, that I may decree tablets of destines of the great gods, he decreed the destiny for him."

Here we see that Fu Xi is relative to one of the Apkallu, or Seven Sages of Enki, who appeared as half man, half fish. The Apkallu were said to dispatch the "me" among mankind. Fu Xi is said to have received the principles of the eight trigrams, which were given to him by the Emperor in Heaven, the Jade Emperor, who ranks slightly below the Three Pure Ones. The fact that the Tablets of Destiny were associated with the *mes* is supported by the work of Sarah Barlett. In the book, *A Brief History of Angels and Demons,* she writes on page 44:

"In Sumerian mythology, Inanna stole the Tablets of Destiny, the Me (pronounced 'mai'), from Enki,"

Here we see that Fu Xi is one of the Seven Sages of ancient Mesopotamian lore. Also that the Yi Jing is what the ancient Mesopotamians would call the Tablets of Destinies. What started off as the eight trigrams, or bagua, would develop into a system of sixty-four hexagrams by the time of the legendary Yu the Great, whose estimated rule in China spanned from 2194 B.C.E. – 2149 B.C.E. Ironically, Yu the Great was noted to have introduced "flood control" in China. The system of sixty-four hexagrams is quite similar to the sixty-four Sumerian mes that made up the Tablets of Destinies. Based on our discussion thus far, it seems remarkably evident that the Tablet of Destines was indeed the Yi Jing, but there is something very important that we have to take into consideration.

The Cult of Nyarzir

One thing about the history of the Yi Jing that should not be overlooked, which I will spend a brief time on, is that it compares greatly with the Ifa system of divination. The connection here is that many of the people living in West Africa are descendants of the Sumerians, and the Sumerians did migrate from a region near the Pacific Ocean. Ifa is the only religion, a primordial one, that has a continuing story of the goddess Ishtar. It is said that the Yoruban deity Oshun, wore a white dress at one time, but the dress turned yellow because of having to wash it over and over again. Her children were also taken away from her due to the Orishas dissatisfaction in her activities of prostitution. Ishtar's sacred color is white, and distinctly different than most Venusian deities, she is the Lady of Sacred Prostitution. Connections between ancient Mesopotamia and West Africa were known in the ancient world. The following references are useful in further illustrating this point:

"(History of Ethiopia, Vol. I., Preface, by Sir E. A. Wallis Budge.) **In addition Budge notes that, "Homer and Herodotus call all the peoples of the Sudan, Egypt, Arabia, Palestine and Western Asia and India Ethiopians." (Ibid., p. 2.) Herodotus wrote in his celebrated History that both the Western Ethiopians, who lived in Africa, and the Eastern Ethiopians who dwelled in India, were black in complexion, but that the Africans had curly hair, while the Indians were straight-haired."**

The point here is that what is known as Ifa today, existed in ancient Mesopotamia, which leads us to a very important part of our discussion, one that is often overlooked by scholars of the Yi Jing. Anyone who is initiated in a magical or spiritual system can attest to the fact that it is quite foolish, and dangerous to say the least, for the novice to dabble in the occult arts. It is said by some, that the Yi Jing as we know it today, was influenced by the Ifa tradition. In the Ifa tradition, one has to be *initiated to divine the fates*. Earlier in our discussion, we pointed out that the Yi Jing and the Sumerian Tablets of Destinies were one and the same. The Sumerian gods, not only read the fates using the Tablets of Destiny, but employed its technology. The Sumerian deities had a way of employing the power of the Tablets of Destinies. In the same manner, the Yi Jing is not just a system of fates, but also sorcery. If there is an initiatory system of Ifa divination, it should be expected that one should exist for the I Ching as well. This is how the Yi Jing was used in the Cult of Nyarzir.

The first mention of the term Nyarzir occurs in the Gilgamesh Epics. Margaret E. Harkness, in her classic work entitled, *Assyrian Life and History*, published in 1883, recounts the legend of Ziusudra found in the Chaldean version, where he is called by the Hellenized version of his name, Xisuthrus. On page 54, we read:

"Xisuthrus opens the window of his ark, and looks forth. On all sides he sees desolation, corpses floating upon the waters, and no sign of dry land. Finally the ark rests on the mountain of *Nizir*, "the mountain of the world," which the Accadians believed to be the cradle of their race, like another Olympus, the habitation of the gods."

Here we see that the Mountain of Nizir, from which the term Nyarzir is founded upon, was believed to be the origin of the Chaldean race and the home of the gods. According to the ancient Mesopotamians, it was only the "gods" who knew how to employ the powers of the Tablets of Destinies. These "gods" were Sorcerers of the Yi Jing. But, how can we be sure that there was indeed a migration from the "Empire of Mu" into ancient Mesopotamia?

Where Did the Yi Jing Originate?

Barbara G. Walker reveals some very valuable information concerning the Yi Ching, in her book, *The I Ching of the Goddess*. On page 14 of the said work, she writes:

"Older Asian systems attributed to the Goddess, not the God, every type of logical system for expressing cycles of time and space, including calendars, time measurements by astrological observation...It was said that Fu His was the god as a brother-consort of this primal Goddess who brought all things into being and delegated some of her authority to him....The story that the Goddess gave the I Ching to the cultural hero points to the likelihood that this symbol system- like other systems of ideograms, numbers, calendars, alphabets, measurements, and hieroglyphics- was originated by women in a matriarchal age, when men served chiefly as hunters, warriors, and field hands while women evolved more civilized skills."

Barbara G. Walker, in the information cited above, states that knowledge of the Yi Jing was transmitted from Nuwa to Fu Xi. Nuwa was known in ancient Chinese mythology as a creator deity. Some even consider her to be the first ruler of China. Is it really possible that Fu Xi could have gotten such knowledge from Nuwa? It seems very probable and may lead us into another discovery. If the Tablets of Destiny is indeed the Yi Jing, and the evidence does indeed point to such, then ancient

Mesopotamian records should support Barbara G. Walker's observation. In the *Babylonian Creation Epic*, we read:

"She exalted Kingu; in their midst she raised him to power.
To march before the forces, to lead the host,
To give the battle-signal, to advance to the attack,
To direct the battle, to control the fight,
Unto him she entrusted; in costly raiment she made him sit, saying:
I have uttered thy spell, in the assembly of the gods I have raised thee to power.
The dominion over all the gods have I entrusted unto him.
Be thou exalted, thou my chosen spouse,
May they magnify thy name over all of them the Anunnaki."
She gave him the Tablets of Destiny, on his breast she laid them, saying:
Thy command shall not be without avail, and the word of thy mouth shall be established."
Now Kingu, thus exalted, having received the power of Anu,
Decreed the fate among the gods his sons, saying:
"Let the opening of your mouth quench the Fire-god;
Whoso is exalted in the battle, let him display his might!"

The Babylonian Creation Epic supports the fact that the knowledge of the Yi Jing (Tablets of Destinies) was in the possession of a feminine force (Tiamat) and then passed over to (Kingu) man. While it is known that the ancient application of the Yi Jing was employed by the use of oracle bones and tortoise shells, what is not often mentioned is that the earliest oracle bone inscriptions are filled with references about the *"wu,"* a term meaning shaman, but in ancient China it meant *female shaman*. Max Dashu, in an article entitled *Wu: Ancient Female Shamans of Ancient China*, writes:

"The shamanic character wu also appears in many compound words, combined with other radicals signifying woman, old woman, male, spirit and immortal."

We can learn something a bit deeper by if we look into the origin of the name of Fu Xi's wife, *Nuwa*. It is well known that female shamans held positions of authority during the matriarchal age. The name Nuwa is composed of two parts, *Nu*, meaning female and *Wa*, the ancient name for Japan. This would mean that the brother-sister, sibling marriage between Fu Xi and Nuwa is symbolic of an era when China and Japan were ruled by a joint force. Nuwa, or Lady of Japan bestowed the knowledge of the Yi Jing to China. This can be confirmed in ancient Mesopotamian mythology as well.

Earlier in our discussion, we made a comparison between Fu Xi and the Sumerian Noah, Ziusudra. Additionally, we found that Fu Xi also compared greatly to the Apkallu. Now before proceed any further, it is good to remember that Japan from times of remote antiquity has been known as the

Land of the Rising Sun. *Quests of the Dragon and Bird Clan* by Paul Kekai Manansala, makes an interesting point about the Mesopotamian legendary city of DIlmun. Manansala writes on page 48:

"The entrance to both the underworld and skyworld was found on Mt. Mashu in Dilmun in the Sea of the Rising Sun. Enki would send fish-being sages known as abgal (Akkadian apkallu) from Dilmun to advise the king-priests."

If Fu Xi was one of the Apkallu, which the evidence does support him as being, then he came from Dilmun. Dilmun is described very much like an area existing in the vicinity of Japan, which seems to be a reference to the Empire of Mu, located around or in the Pacific Ocean. Michael Rice, in a book entitled, *Egypt's Making: The Origins of Ancient Egypt 5000-2000 BCE*, states:

"In Sumerian texts which celebrate Dilmun various epithets are customarily attached to it, by which it is represented as a paradisial place where the gods dwelt and in which numerous act of creation took place. It is called the Land of Crossing, the Land where the Sun Rises (for the Land is situated in the Sea of the Rising Sun) and throughout its literature particular emphasis is placed on Dilmun's purity.."

In ancient Sumerian texts, Dlmun is described as "the Land where the Sun Rises," which is situated in the "Sea of the Rising Sun." It was also described by the Sumerians, like the *Mountain of Nizir* among the Chaldeans, as a land where the gods dwelt and a place of creation. This doesn't discount that there may have been a Dilmun of later ages near the region of ancient Mesopotamia. However, the paradisiacal place of Dilmun where the gods dwelt seems to point to the Empire of Mu located in the region of Japan. If this is the case, then evidence of such should also exist in Eastern, and more specifically, ancient Japanese mythology. Is it possible that the battle described in the Babylonian Creation epic between Marduk and Tiamat, may have been a battle that occurred in the Empire of Mu over sovereignty?

The Tablets of Destiny & The Empire of Mu

The Babylonian Creation epic is quite different than the Sumerian account of creation. In Sumerian mythology, it is Nammu who gave birth to the first gods and comes up with the idea of creating human beings with the help of Enki. In Babylonian mythology, the god Ea (Enki), attacks the primal god Apsu after discovering his plot to kill the younger gods for making too much noise. This is followed by a battle between the older and the younger gods. Marduk, son of the god Ea, is chosen by the younger gods to fight against the older gods. Marduk defeats the primal gods, Kingu and then Tiamat. We can tell that the Sumerians were a different people than the Babylonians, due to the differences found in their perspective creation myths. While many have theorized that the

Babylonian Creation epic was more about promoting Marduk as the supreme god of ancient Mesopotamia, it may very well be possible that these events recorded in this particular mythology reflect a conflict and descent occurring in the prehistoric Empire of Mu.

The idea of a younger god rebelling against an older one, does occur in the ancient mythologies of Japan, specifically between Amaterasu-Ohmikami and her younger brother Susanowo-no-Mikoto. The rivalry between Amaterasu-Ohmikami and her younger brother, Susanoo, is a very popular Shinto myth. Susanoo bears a striking resemblance to the Babylonian god Ea. Both are associated with water. Susanoo is the god of the sea and a trickster deity. Ea is the god of water among other things. Susanoo, like the younger gods in the Babylonian Creation epic, upset the "older gods" by making too much noise. In the case of ancient Japanese mythology, however, we get an idea as to what this noise symbolized. *Nihongi: Chronicles of Japan from the Earliest Times to A.D. 697*, translated by W. G. Aston, [2]gives us this account concerning Susanoo:

"Their next child was Sosa no wo no Mikoto...This God had a fierce temper and was given to cruel acts. Moreover he made a practice of continually weeping and wailing. So he brought many of the people of the land to an untimely end. Again he caused green mountains to become withered. Therefore the two Gods, his

[2] First Turtle edition published in 1972

parents, addressed Sosa no wo no Mikoto, saying: "Thou art exceedingly wicked, and it is not meet that thou shouldst reign over the world. Certainly thou must depart far away to the NetherLand."

If we took Susanoo as the Babylonian Ea, we could now understand that the "noise" which upset the older gods in the Babylonian Creation epic, was indeed acts of malice and the misuse of power. Based on such, Susanoo (Ea) was banished to the Netherland or a region that existed outside the gates of heaven, outside of Dilmun, where the Sumerian gods claimed origin from.

Susanoo's association with the Babylonian Ea is not unfound idea. In the Nihongi, translated by W. A. Aston, Aston defines the name Susanoo:

"Susa no wo is therefore simply "the male of Susa.""

Susa was an ancient city in Mesopotamia and closely associated with Elam. This shows us that there was indeed a difference between the older Afro-Asiatic gods and the younger Mesopotamian gods. The priesthood of the god Ea, like Susanoo, was banished from the Land of the Rising Sun and took up residence in Mesopotamia, in Elam.

This information is also supported by the legendary Kenneth Grant, a direct student of Aleister Crowley. Grant wrote the following in his classic work, *Outer Gateways*:

"Tiamat will once more rule the Earth". Her other number, 71, is the number of Lam, and of the Kami, a name bestowed in ancient Japan upon the Old Ones whom the Egyptians named the Sami."

If Tiamat were indeed the Kami, as Grant suggests, then this would also imply that the Kami were the original holders of the Tablets of Destiny, like Tiamat. We discovered earlier in our discussion that the Yi Jing and the Tablets of Destinies were one and the same.

The Eight Trigrams of the Yi Jing

(Below) The Sumerian Cuneiform Sign for Divinity

Is the Yi Jing (Tablets of Destinies) of Japanese Origin?

During our discussion so far, we have established that the Yi Jing and the Tablets of Destinies are one and the same. We have also explored, and provided evidence for, an existing cult that existed before ancient Mesopotamia and migrated from Dilmun, also known as the Land of the Rising Sun. Kenneth Grant wrote that Tiamat is the Kami of ancient Shinto mythology. We should keep in mind that in many mythologies around the world, there existed a Matriarchal Era, a time when women led society. We can see this in the Babylonian Creation epic and from our discussion of the work of Barbara G. Walker. Grants associates Tiamat with the deities of Japan, which would mean that these were the original holders of the Tablets of Destinies or Yi Jing. First, we must establish that women did in fact take on roles of leadership in prehistoric Japan.

Religion in Japan: Unity & Diversity by H. B. Earhart, makes the following observation in support of the fact that Japan began as a matriarchal society. On page 29 it states:

"For example, the earliest surviving records about Japan are Chinese accounts suggesting both female rulers and female shamans, and the oldest Japanese chronicles also include ruling queens

**who performed religious functions as
divine oracles."**

Historical evidence in regards to Japan's
matriarchal origins is not hard to discover,
especially since it is one of the remaining few
cultures that revere the sun as a goddess, even in
our modern times. While there were the female
shamans who ruled early China, possibly from
their thrones in the Empire of Mu, or pre-historic
Japan, the popularity of such can be determined by
how these practices have survived in modern times
and in what areas.

It seems very probable that Dilmun was indeed
located in the Pacific, "the Sea of the Rising Sun,"
and Japan had close connection to such, or was
Dilmun itself. These ideas, which are well
supported by the evidence presented thus far, were
also known to Asian scholars. Hirata Atsutane[3],
also known by the literary name Ibukinoya, was
ranked as one of the four great men of kokugaku
(nativist) studies and one of the most versed
theologians of Shinto. He was born to a samurai
family of Akita domain. In the work entitled, *The I
Ching in the Shinto Thought of Tokugawa Japan*,
author Wai-ming Ng, writes extensively about
Atsutane's views on the I Ching and its origins:

**"In his later years, Atsutane became deeply
interested in the I Ching and established his own
views on the text. His most original and**

[3] Hirata Atsutane (October 6th, 1776 to November 2nd, 1843)

significant idea on Confucian-Shinto relations was perhaps his distinction between the Chou I and the I Ching. He came up with the idea that the I Ching was not an alien work of literature but the handiwork of a Japanese deity. He wrote the Saneki yuraiki (The origins of the early three versions of the I Ching) (1835) and Taiko koekiden (The I Ching of the ancient past) (1836) to trace the alleged Shinto origins of the ancient I Ching. Turning the honji suijaku theory upside down, he argued that all sage-kings and deities in ancient China were from Japan. For example, Fu Hsi was actually a Shinto deity named Omono-nushi-no-kami, who was supposedly the creator of the trigrams, I Ching charts, oracle bones, and Chinese characters. He asserted that "Later, our god, Omono-nushi-no-kami, also called Taiko-fukki-shi, granted [the Chinese] the Hot'u and Lo shu (Writings from the River Lo), and created the wonderful trigrams... . Based on the images of oracle bones, he invented Chinese characters."

Based on Atsutane's words, we can see that the idea of the Yi Jing originating in Japan is nothing new. However, Atsutane was probably unaware of the Sumerian civilization, as he lived before the time when the world of archeology would discover such. His perspective, however, can be validated by the ancient Sumerian accounts. Since 1978 the Japan Petroglyph Society have found no less than 3000 rocks with engravings throughout Japanese islands, documented by Government of Education and Cultures and Boards of Education. Amazingly, the petroglyphs found on this rocks could only be

deciphered using the Sumerian language.
Xpeditions Magazine.Com reported:

"It is to be noted that most of those 3000 engraved
rocks are located in the precincts or at the
summits of sacred hills, which have been
worshipped by the native inhabitants probably
since prehistoric ages…The engraved stone
tablets shown in photographs above were
excavated at one of sanctuaries in Okinawa and
are kept at the Governmental Museum of
Okinawa prefecture, where since prehistoric ages
about 12000 B.P. to 6500 B. P. "Sobata sea –
people" used to dwell and build peculiar
Okinawan cultures. ..As seen in the pictures, 2 big
birds are engraved at the top of buildings
(perhaps ancient types of shrines) and at the
lower part of each building…In the right stone –
tablet at the lower right is a pyramid engraved.
These will show a characteristic of Japanese
petroglyphs and their religious sides, because
even today at Okinawa native sea people have
sincere faith and pious belief in the legendary
homeland, "Nidai-Kanai" which is believed to
have been located in a very far place in the ocean,
where their ancestors lived happy life forever.
Some scholars suppose that their legendary
homeland must be the lost, sunken continent of
Mu. We do not know exactly when the continent
of Mu sank, but according to undersea
archaeology, some kind of geological catastrophe
must have happened in 12000 B.P. These dates
correspond to the legendary Okinawan stories.

The stone tablets tell complete stories of the Mu's culture and religion at that time. These 12 stone tablets, kept at the Governmental Museum, will provide us clue's to solve the enigmatic origins of human letters and languages. Another characteristic of the Japanese petroglyphs is that 30% of them could be deciphered with Proto-Sumerian and Sumerian cuneiforms. We do not know exactly why Japanese petroglyphs are related with Sumerian letters. The only thing we could suppose is that in the late prehistoric ages, Sumerian seafaring tribes threatened by Akkadians invasions fled to the seas. Some tribes reached prehistoric Japan, which the scholars who belong to The Epigraphic Society of Harvard University used to suggest at the ISAC and E.S. conference. Emeritus Prof. Barry Fell (late President of E.S.) was an outstanding leader of the theory, adding that he is sure the Sumerian seafaring people reached the Far East while other groups reached the Americas B.C...Shown below are exact samples of petroglyphs, which could be deciphered using the Sumerian language."

The Appearance of the Jade Maidens

The Yi Ching Apocrypha of Genghis Khan begins with a section entitled The Song of the Jade Maidens. In Asian mythology, the Jade Maidens act as messengers of the goddess and teachers of Taoist mystics. They impart mystic revelations and present divine foods to those blessed to attend the banquet of the goddess. They are closely associated with Xi Wangmu, the Western Mother, who they reside with, in Kunlun Mountain. This is the same mountain that Fu Xi and his wife Nuwa made petition to the "Emperor of Heaven" after the flood.

Interestingly, the goddess Xi Wangmu is also associated with Nuwa. She "governs the internal structure of the nine heavens and regulates yin and yang," and has domain over the Big Dipper. This would make her closely connected with the Vasuh language, appearing in the Ivory Tablets of the Crow.

The Legend of Genghis Khan

Much has been written in history about the controversial figure Genghis Khan. Some scholars consider him to be the world's greatest military leader and strategist. He established the largest land empire in history. Many people were slaughtered in the course of Genghis Khan's invasions, but he also granted religious freedom to his subjects, encouraged the use of paper money and created the first international postal system.

While the military exploits of Genghis Khan is very well documented, what is often overlooked is his shamanistic practices. In a book entitled, *Shamanism*, by Piers Vitebsky, we read:

"One shaman, who had the power of sitting naked in the middle of a frozen river and melting the ice with his body heat, told the warrior Temujin that the sky god willed Temujin to be master of the world. The shaman gave this warrior the title Genghis Khan. But Genghis was also able to fall into trance and divine the future for himself without any help. When the shaman later changed sides and prophesied that Genghis's younger brother would depose him, Genghis had the shaman put to death. The shaman's body lay in the tent for three days and on the third day rose up through the smoke-hole to the sky, No more was more was heard of him and political ambitions of his faction were broken."

Brenda Lange, in the book, *Genghis Khan*, states:

"Some believe that Genghis Khan was a shaman because of his propensity to climb to the top of the nearest mountain to pray whenever he received bad news or tragedy struck."

Khan also expressed interest in Taoism. Founder of the Dragon Gate sect of Taoism, Changchun zi, had been invited to satisfy the interest of Genghis Khan in "the philosopher stone" and the secret medicine of immortality. He explained the Taoist philosophy and the many ways to prolong life and was honest in saying there was no secret medicine of immortality. Genghis Khan honored him with the title "Spirit Immortal." Genghis also made

Changchun in charge of all religious persons in the empire.

There is another interesting aspect that could explain why Genghis Khan's understanding of the Yi Jing was valuable interest to the Black Dragon Society. Jonathan Clements, in the book, A Brief History of the Samurai, states:

"In the greatest irony of all, a folktale sprang up that claimed the great hero Yoshitsune had not died in the tragedy of Takadachi fort. Instead, there were whispers in Japan that he had fled the country that betrayed him and sought sanctuary on the Asian mainland. There, he had found a willing army of loyalists, who proclaimed him their 'Great Leader.' Under this name, Genghis Khan in Mongol, he had led a mighty army that had conquered much of the known world."

It is believed by some in Japan, especially the Ainu people, that the legendary Samurai, Minamoto no Yoshitsune, actually escaped his demise, eventually beginning a new legacy in Mongolia as Genghis Khan.

The Black Dragon Society

In the early-1900's, Ryochei Uchida founded the paramilitary group in Japan known as the Black Dragon Society. The aims of the Black Dragon Society evolved mainly around the preservation of Japanese culture by "any means necessary." Paul

Manansala, in his book, *Quests of the Dragon and Bird Clan*, writes the following about the history of the Black Dragon Society:

"In Japan, descendants of the Samurai warrior class formed the Black Ocean and later the Black Dragon Society to protect the emperor and traditional Japanese culture. The Black Dragon Society was always at odds with the secular government and suffered numerous crackdowns before the start of World War II. These societies saw Western influence and expansion as the main culprit eroding traditional Japan and continually aimed at curbing this influence.

When the Black Dragon Society condemned Japan's ally Italy for invading Ethiopia, the government nearly crushed the organization.

However, the group was able to influence movements in the U.S. in various ways. One secret organization known as the Pacific Movement of the Eastern World had established close links with Marcus Garvey's Universal Negro Improvement Association, and seems to have had real links with the society."

While the Black Dragon Society was popularly known for its alternative political outlook, the group also investigated occult phenomena. Many members subscribed to the Onmyodo teachings, which were a mixture of Buddhism, Shinto and Taoism.

The Yi Jing Apocrypha of Genghis Khan

The Art of Ninzuwu is the art of Yi Jing magic and initiation. This is a rare path that requires virtue, sincerity and love for the art. The Yi Jing Apocrypha of Genghis Khan in not only a system of divination, but of initiation and magical practice. The first initiation is given in the Ivory Tablets of the Crow. The Ivory Tablets is a mystical text that gives instruction in the proper use of the Vasuh language and the Yi Ching itself. The Yi Jing Apocrypha of Genghis Khan is the second initiation into the miraculous work, a very transformational system indeed.

Those who are not Initiates of Yi Ching sorcery can still use the book, like any other Yi Jing version to gain insight into a certain matter or what have you. There are many formulas that can be performed. This text may take the reader quite some time to absorb. Yi Jing sorcery is a very unique system.

The Art of Ninzuwu is a growing tradition and a path beneficial for those who aspire towards personal and spiritual evolution. The Editor assumes no responsibility for anyone who attempts the rituals listed herein. I wish you all the best in your endeavors.

Messiah'el Bey (Warlock Asylum)

Song of the Jade Maidens

Know that while the things in this world may appear to change, they are still in the same place. A glance between the creator and creation is the cause of time. Things appear to change, but they are still in the same place. Once consciousness is born the cycle ends and that which is aware no longer finds salvation in temples of prayer. Heaven is the condition of our spirits. What crimes have we allowed to exist in the cities and villages of our minds? Surely, these populations live in fear for this is how the world is judged. When the abundance of wickedness that permeates within the mind destroys the spirit, the world will no longer exist. Immortality for us is the act of preventing a dark cloud from entering the residence of the soul, allowing the spirit a peaceful place to heal while basking in the light of eternity.

Remember, it is forbidden to call the creator a god. Gods are kept alive by the same elements that give life to demons. And this force is made abundant by the fire that exists beyond the worlds of light and darkness.

This sacred knowledge has been preserved in the Ivory Tablets of the Crow. The Nine Books of Dreams are a straight line that all circles of phenomena must pass. Many who say they understand these things still have much to learn. Is not life itself an initiation? For this reason those who walk along the path are said to follow a crooked road, a journey in life that shapes the stones of destiny. The Spirit of the Ninzuwu will pass into thy person during the Baptism of the Ancient One and there will appear the Jade Books of Heaven before thee. These Books are nothing more than the Nine Dreams of Nyarzir and these Nine Books cannot be read. It is a formula of the spirit that can only be read when the spirit remembers itself. These Nine Dreams can only be remembered and this is how the world is understood. Know that while the things in this world may appear to change, they are still in the same place.

The beauty of the journey is very hard to capture in words. Its meaning is like the waters of the Fahmu. I began to understand the Nine Books of Dreams more deeply, shortly after my Baptism. I was led to the Fountain of Life by the Shamuzi who explained such knowledge to me in Dreams that were sent by Johuta. Alas, I now understood the Footprints of the Crow and how the Nine Books of Dreams can be invoked.

Know that while the things in this world may appear to change, they are still in the same place. Remember that thy spirit is the feet of the soul firmly planted on the throne. It is the path of the stars in heaven walking around The Crow. Know that events in life also walk around The Crow like the stars in heaven and there are

many Crows perched in the celestial trees. Every galaxy
has a Crow in its center. Surely, the Crow is the Soul. It
is said that even Johuta is a Crow.

Remember, the Goddess Johuta is the Sun behind the
Sun and likened to a mirror. While its light perceives
things as they are, some things are inverted and strange.
Know that the Crow will appear in a certain form to
those whose spirits are not alive. The initiated will see
and understand other manifestations of the Crow. They
may appear at times as a dark space, which the stars
circle around. Yet, on the other side of this dark space,
they appears as a black sphere of great radiance amidst a
white sky.

Shortly after the Baptism of the Ancient One, my spirit
entered Nyarzir and began to remember these things.
Though they appear strange in this place, it is no more
indifferent than the events of the world of man. It was
then that the Bride of Nyarzir revealed the sign of the
Ninzuwu to me. I inscribed it upon the Stone Bowl of
Eternity, and the passages in the Ivory Tablets of the
Crow I understood with great clarity. Soon after these
things occurred, the knowledge of the Nine Books of
Dreams came to me, a gift from Johuta for all those who
seek the path of life and freedom, the necessary
knowledge. And this is the symbol of the Ninzuwu given
to me by the Bride of Nyarzir:

The Yi Jing Apocrypha of Genghis Khan

"The Ninzuwu have the stature of a man and that of a woman. It is a mysterious race. Their height is over twelve feet tall and in front they appear as a woman, and when they turn about, thou will see a face and body of a man upon their backside. They carry no emotion and walk with bright copper skin and white wings that extend the length of a man's arm." – The Ivory Tablets of the Crow

This is the symbol of operation for the Ninzuwu. Many things have been written about the Sword of the Ninzuwu, but it is not known in such a manner. During the Age of the Gods it was said:

"Of old, Heaven and Earth were not yet separated, and the In and Yo not yet divided. They formed a chaotic mass like an egg which was of obscurely defined limits and contained germs. The purer and clearer part was thinly drawn out, and formed Heaven, while the heavier and grosser element settled down and became Earth. The finer element easily became a united body, but the consolidation of the heavy and gross element was accomplished with difficulty. Heaven was therefore formed first, and Earth was established subsequently. Thereafter divine beings were produced between them."

Experience is the only form of prayer for the Ninzuwu. Let the sight of such be held in the mind, on the prominent place of thy altar. Afterwards, recite the Hymn of Ninzuwu:

Priests and Priestesses of Ninzuwu come!
From the Dream of the Great Circle of Stars come!
Ninzuwu, Realm of the Foretelling Knowledge, open!
Ninzuwu, Realm of Divining the thoughts of Planets and Stars, open!
Dream of the Sacred Mirror come upon me!
Ninzuwu, Winged Ministers of the Stars, come!
Ninzuwu, Rulers of the Seven Planets teach me your Ways!

Ninzuwu, Counselors of the Zodiac, come!
I call the Ninzuwu in Love and Honor!
Share with me the Sword of Knowing!
Share with me the Sword of One Who Can Divine the
Thoughts of Others!
I ask for the Gift of the Sword in Purity of The Dream!
Moo-ah-eehzz-oot-you-mmh-ha-moo-ah; eehzz-you-mmh-
ha-moo-ah-eek-hss; oot-eek-hss-oot-eehzz; eh-ph-eh-ph-eek-
hss-moo-ah-oot; you-mmh-ha-whoo-nn-bee-oot-eh-ph.

Ninzuwu with the Dream of Anointing, come!

Remember, that the Ninzuwu are the Caretakers of the
Stars in this Space and the other. The Art of Ninzuwu is
a sacred form of magic. The Ninzuwu are the Magicians
of the Yi Jing. These secrets are not known among the
masses of mankind, as they make inquiry into such
without initiation and fall victim to the spirits of the
dead posing as benevolent caretakers. Remember what is
written in the Ivory Tablets of the Crow:

Man was lost.
The Sons of Aho created a lie.
They posed as the creators of man
But the world is the creator
Made by the creator
And so, man is lost.

The Son of Aho are the emotions of the dead
After the spirit has left the body

Thus, the journey begins with a circle

The Yi Jing Apocrypha of Genghis Khan

With a circle the journey never ends
This is the question of man
For he will never understand the answer.

Take special care to preserve our heritage and our race
among the societies of men. The Ninzuwu are the
Magicians of the Yi Jing. This is a rare art and should
not be confused with the magic of mankind. It is written
in the Ivory Tablets of the Crow:

*"And surely the Magicians of the Secret Lands, not known to
men, study well these words, and those who observe them. Take
special care not to change these instructions that I give unto thee
by one letter, for in its perfection is its initiation."*

They are surrounded by the mystical lands of the Lewhu,
also known as Iewhu. The Lands of Lewhu are eight in
number with a specific formula for each. This is the
Jade Elixir. Lewhu is the eighth letter in the Vasuh
language, as it represents the eight paths leading to the
sixty-four cities of Nyarzir. Know that Lewhu is
Nyarzir. It is written in the Ivory Tablets of the Crow,
concerning Lewhu:

*"It is the eighth letter in the language of Vasuh. It is used in
initiating one to the divine energies of the stars."*

Remember that during the time of initiation, Lewhu is
the Gate that resides over the sexual organs and the
energies thereof. Do not miscalculate the Gate of Lewhu
with lust, but know that this form of sexual energy
radiates from the stars, emissaries of the creator are
what gods are. The Food of the Crow is nourishment for
the Soul. When I visited the Magicians of the West, the
Workers of Mankind, being men themselves, they would
often say marvelous things about the Tree of Life, which
is armed with thirty-two roads. Yet, the land of Nyarzir
has eight cities and sixty-four roads, and the number of

the Ninzuwu will always be twice this amount for the Magicians of Nyarzir speak in a language known in the other universe, a tongue beyond the worlds of darkness and light. The Tongue of the Ninzuwu is the spark by which the Yi Jing moves and can be employed. It is written in the Ivory Tablets of the Crow:

"Now the Nyarzir is a world with Three Suns and a Green Sky. Every structure is made out of a precious jewel and the roads of the cities are as fine metals. And these cities all stand around the Shining Trapezohedron upon which the Bride of Nyarzir sits upon her Throne."

In the Art of Ninzuwu, it is known that these three suns are written as three horizontal lines, one on top of the other. Accordingly, it is stated in the Age of the Gods:

"Hence it is said that when the world began to be created, the soil of which lands were composed floated about in a manner which might be compared to the floating of a fish sporting on the surface of the water. At this time a certain thing was produced between Heaven and Earth. It was in form like a reed-shoot. Now this became transformed into a God, and was called Kuni-toko-tachi no Mikoto. Next there was Kuni no sa-tsuchi no Mikoto, and next Toyo-kumu-nu no Mikoto, in all three deities. These were pure males spontaneously developed by the operation of the principle of Heaven."

This knowledge we gave to each and every civilization, and each civilization was able to use such knowledge to make life prosperous in their own nation. But the knowledge and initiation that enables the Priest and Priestess to create change in the world is withheld from man, and only those who come from this path are drawn to the path. Stay with the Soul of Fire prayer.

The Lands Of Nudzuchi

There exists the Fire of Heaven in all things, and all things will attract to itself a particular experience, due to the nature of the fire that emanates from all matter, whether it is in motion or still. Know that there was a time when women possessed such knowledge and due to such were able to place in category that which emanated the highest degree of the Flame of Heaven according to its influence over the environment. These things were done so that the said forces could be curbed and cultivated for the benefit of man. Nudzuchi and the Priests and Priestesses of her dominion are teachers of these things. Know that life is the space where the forces of Heaven and Earth constantly migrate back and forth between each other. It was said during the Age of the Gods:

"These make eight Deities in all. Being formed by the mutual action of Heavenly and Earthly principles, they were made male and female. From Kuni no toki-tachi no Mikoto to Izanagi no Mikoto and Izanami no Mikoto are called the seven generations of the Age of the Gods."

This is a science that will always appear strange to men who worship gods of chance. It is due to such worship that men of such stature find themselves under the Laws of Cause and Effect and the Law of Accidents.

Know that while the things in this world may appear to change, they are still in the same place. A glance between the creator and creation is the cause of time. Earth is the Temple of Heaven. It is a space between the worlds of Shki and Zhee, but its nature is that of Hmu.

It is a nourishing place that has eight roads. Some of these paths are easier to endure than others, but all are of great benefit and there is much that can be learned in this time and place. I have kept the formula for those wishing to enter the Land of Nudzuchi, called Kun by some of the Orientals. These instructions are given elsewhere in this writing. However, I will write the words that must be recited here. Now the Opening of the Sea must occur, and the Soul of Fire Prayer and the Calling of the Shamuzi. These are the words and they must be recited six times in front of the Wutzki:

Eek-hss-ooh-wel-eehzz, moo-ah-moo-ah-eehzz-oot, whoo-nn-bee-eehzz,

Nudzuchi-eek-hss-eehzz-eehzz, Kun-eek-hss-eehzz-eehzz

Moo-ah-eehzz-moo-ah-oot, moo-ah-moo-ah-eehzz-oot, you-mmh-ha-eek-hss-moo-ah

Whoo-nn-bee eehzz Nudzuchi, Whoo-nn-bee.

Nudzuchi is the Earth and the Earth is the foundation
of all magic and the unseen magic that exists in life.
Nudzuchi is the Face of the West appearing on the Bride
of Nyarzir. She teaches that the laws of alchemy consist
of three horizontal lines. First, the Magician of Nyarzir
must perform the rite in meditation. Second, the
Magician of Nyarzir must perform a ritual or an
operation of the good work. Third, the Magician of
Nyarzir must take some course of action to reflect the
previous two workings for Heaven is in Earth and Earth
is in Heaven.

Know that when the trigram has been performed, one
must take time to visit the cities connected with the
Land of Nudzuchi and converse with her tradesmen. In
this manner the Magician can see the light of Nudzuchi
in the course of one's life.

In the manner of Nudzuchi, the first horizontal line is
the meditation of Hmu. The second horizontal line is the
rite of the Ayaqox. The third line is the rite of
Nudzuchi, also known as Kun and Di. Know that there
are eight cities that the light of Nudzuchi is able to
reach. The names of these cities I write in this space,
along with the Priests and Priestesses that rule over this
realm.

Second Hexagram

The Land of Orogorojima

Kun

Ruler. Nudzuchi

(Shki) There is a fire in earth, the power which makes plants grow. This fire also exists in heaven. (Lewhu) Six broken lines making twelve lines. The Earth is the ground upon which the animals of the zodiac walk upon. (Zhee)Earth is the hard fire of Heaven, the solid light of the goddess.

The Second Letter of Genghis Khan to the Magicians of the Yi Jing:

Entering the road of immortality is not an easy task. One must first become a symbol. Symbols have their voices heard in Heaven and on Earth. But in understanding the Earth, the Ninzuwu begins to understand the symbol of Heaven. The Earth will always attract Heaven to itself. Once the courtship of Heaven and Earth begins, many marvelous things are created. If a man wants to create a foundation for himself, he must first learn the language of Heaven. He must then learn to listen to Heaven. He must practice the Law of Heaven on Earth. It is in this manner that he begins to understand the Earth, for Earth is his mother. Earth is his first teacher.

Earth is the body of a woman. There are twelve parts to a woman's body like the signs of Heaven. She holds a universe inside of her womb for nine months. She gives birth to Heaven and Heaven responds to the voice of its Mother.

Mother soon disregards anything that is wasted, when what is wasted is sent from Heaven. She cares for her child. Earth feeds Heaven. She teaches Heaven how to walk. She teaches Heaven how to speak. In time, Heaven will leave the house of its Mother. This is the cycle of Heaven and Earth.

Seventh Hexagram

The Land of Ahaji

Shih

Priest: Ahaji

(Zhee) Without discipline the light of the goddess cannot be cultivated. Remember that nothing in life is free, but honesty and respect is the greatest form of payment that can be given. (Shki) Death energy is transformational energy and a degree of integrity is needed or everything will change. (Hmu) Once change occurs, desire begins. Desire is also possession, but can be used as a vehicle of travel. (Nzu)

Learning to protect self and gaining money require the same handshake.

The Seventh Letter of Genghis Khan to the Magicians of the Yi Jing:

Earth is the body of a woman. When she is pregnant, the life inside of her is contained in water. Water is the medium by which she will communicate with her child while it is growing in her womb. During this time of pregnancy, the woman cannot drink beer. She must discipline herself for nine months. All her thoughts are of things concerning the child and in this way she shapes the face of the child. Everything that she eats will be shared with her child, and in this way she shapes the body of the child. Her feelings during the time of pregnancy will create the child's way of thinking. She must have discipline to give birth to life. It is the same with Art of the Ninzuwu. Remember what is written in the Ivory Tablets of the Crow:

"Know that every civilization comes into this world in the manner of the Unborn. Each city exists in a place not known to time and then descends upon the realm of man as a kingdom, through some act of war, or a great migration."

Do not be deceived by the foolish talk of men, for they would like to see many things come to pass during their lifetime. Take heed, not in words, but in the stature of the commander of armies. This is how such things can be accomplished. Life is a battle and its warriors must be armed with the good fortune of persistence in their skill, as these things are heavenly gifts kept in the space of the Moon. The Moon is water in the Earth that makes plants grow.

In the world before time lives the Priest Ahaji. He knows well the art of discipline and teaches the newly-initiated in the manner and customs of the temple

The Yi Jing Apocrypha of Genghis Khan

(Earth.) He indicates all dangers in thy undertakings
and can aid in the study of difficult arts and sciences.

Eleventh Hexagram

The Land of Iyonofutana

Tai

Priestess: Iyonofutana

(Tuu) The science of protection is also the science of healing, and this is the meaning of marriage. (Aum) Peace can only be found when the inner light that resides within begins the process of intercourse with the goddess. (Nzu) When healing life's wounds, love in the end result.

The Eleventh Letter of Genghis Khan to the Magicians of the Yi Jing:

Earth is the body of a woman. There is so much harmony when a man finds a woman who will reveal her interest in him first. During this time, the realm of nature becomes a bed of lovemaking for man and woman. Lovemaking has great success when the woman is on top.

The Yi Jing Apocrypha of Genghis Khan

She can satisfy herself with ease and the man can endure the pleasure much longer. She is free to express herself and willingly cares for her husband when this position occurs. Remember, Earth is a temple, and this can be seen in life. Earth is also the solidified sexual energy preserved through discipline. Success comes with the enjoyment and cultivation of the sexual energy. The lessons of such remain unseen by the uninitiated, but can be seen with much clarity for those who know the path.

Lamshu is a beautiful woman. She is the world of nature. It is better for her to teach us. She is often invoked to improve business and for success in domestic affairs, or to rid oneself of unnecessary blockages. Her name is that of Nudzuchi when she discovered Xuz in the cave. It is written in the Ivory Tablets of the Crow:

"Xuz took refuge in a cave, hoping that the cold wind would cease and fell asleep with only with a day's ration of food left, being that his company abandoned him. He awoke in fear from the sound of approaching footsteps. Shortly after, a woman appeared with a fresh pot of stew in her hands and a drawn sword. She was a beautiful maiden with long black hair and full lips, like the flowers that last for one season. The woman spoke to Xuz in a language that he could not understand. She sat down next to Xuz and fed him the stew with one hand while holding the sword to his throat with the other. But when Xuz revealed himself to her, the woman was astonished to see a man with black skin. She trembled with fear, thinking that he might be an emissary from the other worlds. She withdrew her sword and stayed with him for some time. She taught him the mysterious language of the Orientals and their knowledge of certain plants and how to heal the body."

Fifteenth Hexagram

The Land of Oki

Ch'ien

Priest: Oki

(Zhee) The light of the goddess is unseen by man, yet it nurtures our growth and does not take any reward in the form of praise. (Bnhu) There is wealth that is hidden. All the legends of finding a hidden treasure required humility. The voice of Earth will not speak in honor of itself because such things are forbidden in the Earth. Remember, the Earth is a temple and one must enter the temple with humility. We are everything in our minds and nothing in the world we live in.

The Fifteenth Letter of Genghis Khan to the Magicians of the Yi Jing:

Earth is the body of a woman. There is great honor in childbirth, but it is an act of humility for the woman.

The Yi Jing Apocrypha of Genghis Khan

She must unclothe herself and the stranger will see her nakedness. Her face will turn ugly from pain during childbirth. Her sacred chamber will bleed and appear like an apparition of a demon. She must learn humility before she can hold a new child in her arms.

Earth is the body of a woman. There are twelve parts to a woman's body like the signs of Heaven. She holds a universe inside of her womb for nine months. She gives birth to Heaven and Heaven responds to the voice of its mother. Before the birth of a new Sun, the Earth will forfeit her glory. The leaves will fall from the trees and vegetation will be no more. It is during this time that the Earth is having birth pangs. Her pregnancy begins during the time of the Virgin and a new child is born during the time of the Bull. And the Earth also performs acts of humility before the birth of a new Sun.

Before a man can become a Magician, he must be a Fool. And the Fool will climb the Mountain and experience severe conditions. His face will change shape, like that of a pregnant woman. Once he has reached the top of the mountain the Fool will prepare an altar for himself. He is no longer a Fool, but a Magician.

Wajahz will show thee the road of the hidden treasure, but it is always gained from what is invisible in thy presence. His spirit will lead you without resistance to a place of peace. It is likened to picking up money from off the ground. Zhee-Bnhu means all creatures in the language of our sacred clan. It represents humility, since all creatures are in the same space.

Nineteenth Hexagram

The Land of Tsukushi

Lin

Priestess Tsukushi:

(Phe) Expectation is a tool useful for creating the goal. (Lewhu) There is achievement for those who have ears that can listen to an elder speak. In the Vasuh language, phe-lewhu also means balance.

The Nineteenth Letter of Genghis Khan to the Magicians of the Yi Jing:

The eighth month is not evil when success draws near. Yet, there is a processed involved. Earth is the body of a woman. When she has given birth there is much joy in the house about the baby. However, she must also take care of herself. When the baby arrives, joy will follow and also the afterbirth. The afterbirth is cynical in its approach and a small discrepancy of the success gained.

The Yi Jing Apocrypha of Genghis Khan

The afterbirth is a period of time that is understood best by the nursemaid. Wisdom of the aged woman is sacred. An older woman is a witch by nature and can teach those around her many marvelous things. Tsukushi often appears as the Sensei and is called the Great Comforter.

Twenty-Fourth Hexagram

The City of Sado

$\wp_{\circ}\ \gamma\ \text{\#}\vee\ \text{\#}\vee$

Fu

Priest: Sado

$\wp_{\circ}\ \gamma\ \text{\#}\vee\ \text{\#}\vee$ (Zhee) Light is a cord connecting two points in the medium of time. (Shki) When light enters a dark place, it will stay for some time and return to its source. (Tuu) The breath teaches us in its movement back and forth that there is no trouble in traveling as one pleases. (Tuu) When an experience appears in your life over and over again, it wants to be your friend.

The Twenty-Fourth Letter of Genghis Khan to the Magicians of the Yi Jing:

Earth is the body of a woman. After she has given, birth her belly will begin to return to its normal shape. The woman will go back to her daily chores. It will take some time for things to be as they were, but things are never the same unless an old experience can share in a new beginning. The Earth is over Thunder and a mother knows this well for she will hear the Thunder after the baby has been born. During the night the baby will awaken in its early stages of life. It will begin to cry for it does not understand sleep and is afraid of what it means. The mother will constantly return to the baby and comfort its spirit. This process will continue until the baby becomes familiar with sleep and learns how to stand.

 Know that our dreams will cry during the night, and that we as parents of such ambitions must attend to such things until the dream can stand on its own. We give birth to our dreams and must nurture them until they can stand on their own two feet and walk in this reality. Before this time, the dream will cry like a voice of Thunder and we must return to it constantly and comfort it, perfect its being. When the mind of the dream becomes stronger it will no longer cry for it understands success.

Be cautious in thy undertakings. There are spirits of poverty that also call out to the mind and nothing grows out of these things except spirits of poverty. It is like the stricken soul that constantly returns to the shaman asking for this and asking for that. Eventually, the shaman got tired of the stricken soul returning to him, asking foolish questions. When the stricken soul returned to the shaman again, the shaman led the stricken soul out to a burial field and showed the man that both of their graves were next to each other. If you keep returning to the same answer, you will be buried by the same question. We return to things that are not finished, and when they are finished, they will return to us as a blessing or a curse.

Sado often reveals the benefit of what was once experienced and shows us where it now resides in the new experience.   When Sado is approached inquire only once.

Thirty-Sixth Hexagram

The Land of Tsushima

𝒆𝒐 𝒆𝒓𝒕𝒐 𝒆𝒐 𝒅

Ming-Yi

Priestess: Tsushima

𝒆𝒐 𝒆𝒓𝒕𝒐 𝒆𝒐 𝒅 (Zhee) The fire in the Earth is a great lesson (Lewhu) of initiation. The Fire (Zhee) in the Earth is responsible for pushing plants out of the soil.

The Thirty-Sixth Letter of Genghis Khan to the Magicians of the Yi Jing:

Earth is a body of the woman. After the woman has become accustomed to being a mother and a wife, she learns how to maintain the internal fire of the priestess. Being a mother and a wife, she is no longer the young

69

woman who sought to have her way by shining her beauty among men who willingly offered her favors because of such. She must now cultivate her kingdom without praise or honor. A mother and a wife is a woman who has truly dedicated her life to the creator. It is a task that has no reward. It is a work more sacred than that of the prophets.

She must learn how to fulfill her husband's needs while breastfeeding the baby. Her husband will receive many honors for maintaining a beautiful family, but it is the woman who is the invisible cause of this joy. While her work may seem futile, it is not done in vain. Like the Sun that sets, preparing for the journey into the underworld, the woman focuses on judging the dead, and turning lifeless things into beautiful moments. Her menstruation is the mark of her initiation. It is by such things that she learns how to rule the household through a hidden intelligence that does not threaten her husband's position. These things have been discussed before. It is written in the Ivory Tablets of the Crow:

"After the birth of Johuta, the people in the village began to make gossip, concerning Nudzuchi, and accused her of practicing necromancy, since Johuta, like Xuz, was black. The people began treating Nudzuchi like an evil spirit."

Tsushima increases the use of the intuition, for it is Earth over Fire.

Forty-Sixth Hexagram

The Land of Shinatohenomikoto

4⟩ ℓ⟩ ⨆⟩ ⧺√

Sheng

Priestess: Shinatohenomikoto

4⟩ ℓ⟩ ⨆⟩ ⧺√ (Aum) Call the fire (Zhee) from the emotions (Phe) and it will aid in traveling without the body.

The Forty-Sixth Letter of Genghis Khan to the Magicians of the Yi Jing:

The Earth is the body of a woman. When the woman is secure in her power of ruling the world through unseen methods, menstruation will cease. The wind will come and blow out the fire. Her task is one of peace and learning how to ascend. Rarely, does the wind move from the ground towards heaven, but the breath of a woman knows this art well. The woman will use her breath to speak encouraging words to her husband and children at a distance. The woman will maintain bright thoughts

about her family, even in adverse conditions. She knows
that reality is a result of one's emotional state.
Remember, Earth is the body of a woman and the
emotions are the trees growing out of its soil. These can
be shaped for the success of all.

Pay close attention to the work at hand, for this is the
formula. Know that each trigram is a method of working
the Art of Ninzuwu. Every trigram has its own formula,
but the structure of the work is the same.

Nudzuchi (3rd line)
Ayaqox (2nd line)
Hmu (1st line)

After you have invoked each of the eight lands, one after
another, with its prayer of entrance, these may appear in
your dreams or in the method of divination given later in
this writing. When such occurs you must follow the road
as prescribed. The first line, the line at the bottom of the
trigram, represents one of the Nine Letters in the Vasuh
language, which must be invoked through the nine
wheels. It must rise and descend and rise back to the seat
of Zhee. Its mantra must be vibrated while doing such
with its image fresh in the mind. This practice of Soul of
Fire must be implemented when performing the formula
relating to the second line of the trigram. The formulae
for such is given in the Ivory Tablets of the Crow.
Afterwards, the Ninzuwu must call out to one of the
eight lands, the third line of the trigram with the
formulae appearing with its description.

The Yi Jing Apocrypha of Genghis Khan

Let it also be known that when that when one trigram appears over the other, one must perform the rite of the lower trigram first and then ascend to the ruling trigram. This is known as the Exercise of the Hexagram. Once having obtained a thorough knowledge of such, it can be called by its Priestess, or Priest in thine own temple.

The Yi Jing Apocrypha of Genghis Khan

The Mountains of Xuz

Xuz is the Mountain, the youngest son. He is the
Watcher. When the spirit is on high all the other lands
can be seen. The Mountain is where Heaven and Earth
meet. This is the wisdom of Xuz.

It is a silent land and in silence Xuz can be easily
understood. The Mountain rests upon the Earth. Xuz is
the warrior-priest who is defiant to all things that
occurred before. This is the most essential part of the
initiation.

The Land of Xuz is a mountAinuus land, eight
mountains in total. Its sign consists of five parts. It is the
space of stillness and where one begins to learn the
knowledge of the five elements. The formulae for
entering the Mountains of Xuz is the same as all other
lands, save the words are different. Each letter is a
Dream. These words must be said five times during thy
entrance into the Mountains of Xuz.

I will write the words that must be recited here. Now the
Opening of the Sea must occur, and the Soul of Fire
Prayer and the Calling of the Shamuzi. These are the

words and they must be recited five times in front of the Wutzki:

Whoo-nn-bee –eehzz Xuz! Whoo-nn-bee-eehzz Gen

Xuz!

Whoo-nn-bee –eehzz Xuz! Whoo-nn-bee-eehzz Gen

Xuz!

Whoo-nn-bee –eehzz Xuz! Whoo-nn-bee-eehzz Gen!

Xuz!

Eh-ph-moo-ah-ooh-zz-nn,

you-mmh-ha-eh-ph-oot-whoo-nn-bee-moo-ah-eehzz-eek-

hss-whoo-nn-bee Xuz!

Xuz is an initiation for the Magician. You do not understand my words, for nothing is understood by the voice until one can remember the voice of his own spirit. The voice of the spirit can be heard during the practice of this formula.

Xuz (3rd line)
Quekanuit (2nd line)

The Yi Jing Apocrypha of Genghis Khan

Nzu (1st line)

The method of operation of the formula is explained in the Land of the Mother, Nudzuchi. Follow this map, as it is the Path of Xuz and a key to the eight mountains.

Fourth Hexagram

The Mountain of Ohoyamatsumi

Meng

Priest: Ohoyamatsumi-no-Kami

(Phe) The art of levitation is a skill and useful for the climb, but the spirit must be pure in order to fly. (Tuu) Virtue is a protection in such worlds. (Tuu) The vitality of the body is found in the mind. (Bnhu) Abundance is in the eye of the beholder. Phe-aum-aum-bnhu means dream and to dream is to discover.

The Fourth Letter of Genghis Khan to the Magicians of the Yi Jing:

Earth is the body of a woman and her breasts are a Mountain for the young boy that rests upon them. Pay attention to the course of the young infant. It will seek the food of its mother's breast without anger or jealousy of those who have tasted her milk in prior times. New life does not seek to impress those who have lived longer and remains happy because of such. The spring shooting forth its waters is a blessing before the climb.

Just look at how many prophets have journeyed into the Mountains. They were ordinary men who sought spiritual things, things unseen. It was hard finding a proper road of travel in order to reach such things. They faced the many horrors of the mind and spirit. Upon finding the Path, they must now climb the Mountain made out of everything they sacrificed on the journey to reach it. This is how a Fool becomes a Magician.

Eighteenth Hexagram

The Mountain of Nakayamatsumi

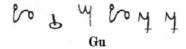

Gu

Priestess: Nakayamatsumi-no-Kami

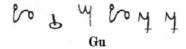 Zhee-bnhu-nzu-zhee-shki-shki means repair. (Zhee) The fire of life changes direction when the mind shifts. (Bnhu) The focus of wealth is found in nature, in care for such, blessings will follow. (Nzu) We must heal what was sacrificed by the skillful use of words. (Zhee) A fire can only burn in clean air. (Shki) Change follows uncleanliness. (Shki) Those who are clean can control change.

The Eighteenth Letter of Genghis Khan to the Magicians of the Yi Jing:

It is the work of the Fool, like the baby that feeds from its mother's breast. It is the work of the Fool. And the

Fool will reach the Mountain of all that he has sacrificed to reach the Path of Knowing. When he has arrived at the foot of the Mountain, he will hear the voice of the wind giving him certain instructions. Above all, he must begin cleaning up the things that he has sacrificed on the journey, which is now the Mountain itself.

Be careful. It is a very difficult way of cleaning. It is ridding the mind of all the things that have caused us to be infatuated with ourselves. The Fool carries all the tools of the Magician. He thinks that he is a Magician because he has traveled on the journey for so long. He has all the tools of the Magician, but does not know how to use them. He came into possession of the Magician's tools because he is the youngest son of the High Priestess like every other Fool. The Fool can only be a Fool. He can be nothing more than a Fool. In order for him to become a Magician, he must first destroy the Fool. Change cannot occur unless something is destroyed and made into something new. The Wind at the foot of the Mountain is different than the Wind at the crown of the Mountain.

When the Fool arrives at the foot of the Mountain, the voice of the Wind will instruct him. It will tell him to clean up the Mountain. This is no easy task for he has neglected so much, which must be amended in the faith of the virtue that was learned on the journey. It is during this process of cleaning that he can destroy the Fool and become a Magician. In cleaning up all that he has sacrificed on the journey, he must begin to use the tools of the Magician.

At first, he may fear the practice of becoming and being a Magician. It is a practice that does not appear similar to the great and wondrous things that he read about in books. When such is the case, you must know that the Fool has not been destroyed. Later, he will begin to measure his actions against the results they produced. When he finds such behavior displeasing, though it may appear pleasing in the eyes of the uninitiated, the Fool is beginning to die.

The Wind, his eldest sister and reflection of his mother, will persist in causing the destruction of the Fool. Such was the case with Xuz. It is written in the Ivory Tablets of the Crow:

"The people began treating Nudzuchi like an evil spirit. So Xuz took his family up to the mountains for a short while, teaching Johuta the wisdom of the lands that he acquired during his journeys, as well as, their mysterious languages, and the unique path that connects many lands, which were unknown to merchants during that time."

The Magician is born when the Fool no longer thinks of himself as a Magician. The Wind at the foot of the Mountain is different than the Wind that blows upon its crown.

Twenty-Second Hexagram

The Mountain of Hayamatsumi

#V ⁴⁄ ⁿ₁ ℓ⁰

Bi

Priest: Hayamatsumi-no-Kami

#V ⁴⁄ ⁿ₁ ℓ⁰ (Tuu) There is beauty in dreams that fly. (Nzu) Begin when the dream is open. (Shki) Changes are only found in objects. (Zhee) The Fire under the Mountain calls for things smaller than the Mountain.

The Twenty-Second Letter of Genghis Khan to the Magicians of the Yi Jing:

When the initiation occurs, and the young man begins to clean up all that he has sacrificed to reach the Mountain, he must use Fire with skill.

It is the same for the baby drawing milk from its mother's breasts. The Fire is the milk and it cannot be greedily consumed by the infant. Otherwise, it will injure the breasts, and the breasts are the Mountain.

The Magician must now work on climbing the Mountain and cleaning up all that he has sacrificed to reach the top of the Mountain. Carefully using the Fire to repair even the smallest thing is a skill and there is much success in this course. It is in these things that he begins to climb the Mountain. His legs will begin to feel the heat of the climb and there is strength in this. Take care of small things and your foundation will be made strong. This is the work of the Magician when he is no longer a Fool.

People pray to the gods to solve the smallest problems and throw their largest burdens up against the altar of chance. When you see this sign, know that they have become infatuated with their own beauty.

Twenty-Third Hexagram

The Mountain of Shikiyamatsumi

Bo

Priestess: Shikiyamatsumi-no-Kami

(Phe) The work of emotions is endless.
(Hmu) Focus on the place where the breath descends, the
still moment.

The Twenty-Third Letter of Genghis Khan to the Magicians of the Yi Jing:

The Art of Ninzuwu breeds clarity of the mind. There
are times when we must remain still, for the world of
emotions is a world of prisons. It is written in the Ivory
Tablets of the Crow:

"There is no sense of reasoning with these feelings. I have seen them possess the body of the unwary, causing fits of anger and all sorts of hypocrisies. And the power these feelings have over the body of man cannot be put into words. But when the spirit is torn from the body these feelings act on their own accord and will haunt another house of flesh."

When the Mountain rests upon the Earth, the Magician will look down and remember his obligation. It is with this knowledge that the Magician must act in a just manner towards those who are still without sight. He must remember that his personality was molded by the experiences he had with the Common-folk and that these people are the ground upon which he stands.

These people are not beggars and will only demand from him the emotions that he acquired during their shared experiences. And the Magician must satisfy their thirst with joy, giving them back more than they requested in return. The Magician must strip away these things and satisfy the demands of the people with great generosity. What is heaven for the Common-folk is hell for the Magician. And what is heaven for the Magician is hell for the Common-folk. This is the ancient Law of Gods and Demons.

Know too, that this Law of Gods and Demons exist in the societies of men and in nature. What is wasted by some is food for the other. The only difference between the Magician and the Common-folk is that the Common-folk allow their ambitions to become their fears. These fears were once goals that were ripe for the harvest, but were left unattended and soon decayed. They now haunt the minds of the people who planted them. The Magician is the cultivator of changes and plants his own ambitions. He has no desire to purchase them at the market like the Common-folk. The Common-folk will always leave what is in his field to buy what grows in his own yard from the marketplace.

The Magician knows not the agony of these things. His generosity to those less fortunate are the bricks that he will build his castle with.

Twenty-Sixth Hexagram

The Mountain of Masakatsuyamatsumi

Da Chu

Priest: Masakatsuyamatsumi-no-Kami

(Zhee) The light of the goddess is never hidden (Nzu) when it dwells in the vicinity of the Mountain.

The Twenty-Sixth Letter of Genghis Khan to the Magicians of the Yi Jing:

The work is never done alone. In the beginning, it may appear as such, for there is wisdom in reflection. When the Magician is engaged in the work, voices from antiquity will call him. Remember what is written in the Ivory Tablets of the Crow:

The Yi Jing Apocrypha of Genghis Khan

"The Ninzuwu know well the Path of Dreams. During these days of Calling, the rays of the Sun will anoint thee. The Ninzuwu may visit the person of these operations in physical form, usually as one ripe in years."

When the spirit begins to awaken, it will remember the words of wisdom from those Magicians of ancient times. While the body of magic is unseen it is alive and will always call its own to itself. Magic is not magic. Magic is the art of cultivation. When our thoughts are with the dark cloud, remember the words of those who ventured forth before you. When you feel angry and the dark cloud is haunting your mind, remember the wise ones who have passed before you. When you practice these things a great harvest is ahead.

Twenty-Seventh Hexagram

The Mountain of Ihasaku

Yi

Priest Ihasaku-no-Kami

(Tuu) Eat the healthy things (Tuu) and you will protect your vitality (Hmu) and immortality.

The Twenty-Seventh Letter of Genghis Khan to the Magicians of the Yi Jing:

Magic is the art of cultivation and in this cultivation is nourishment. One must be aware of the food that enters the body and the mind. During his time in the Mountain, the Magician will nurture his essence and the spirit is his internal infant. When he hears the Thunder, he knows that the infant is in need of nourishment.

The Yi Jing Apocrypha of Genghis Khan

We are always eating. When we are not eating physical
food, we are eating the food of the mind. It is all one
food, but eating in itself is not nourishment.
Nourishment is the man who cultivates the soil knowing
that what he eats is also a place of resurrection in the
mind.

Forty-First Hexagram

The Mountain of Takawo

Sun

Priestess: Takawo-Kami

(Shki) If the one who possess wealth tries to sell the formula, (Bnhu) what they have will decrease.

The Forty-First Letter of Genghis Khan to the Magicians of the Yi Jing:

Make sure that you leave an equal portion of life for life. The Magician can receive the blessing when his cup is empty. When his bowl remains full for too long, it is a sign that what was once gained is being stored. It has been stored for so long that it is being wasted. Remaining with the same thoughts is like the Mountain over the Lake, a breeding place for mosquitos. Diminish what is in the cauldron. It is a new season for new blessings to come.

Fifty-Second Hexagram

The Mountain of Xuz

卅∨ 卅∨

Gen

Ruler: Xuz

卅∨ 卅∨
      (Tuu) Preserve your virtue by protecting yourself against the ways of the world. (Tuu) The purity of your spirit is the gold of life.

The Fifty-Second Letter of Genghis Khan to the Magicians of the Yi Jing:

Those who are skilled in the arts of combat know that with every new war, new muscles must be exercised. If the same thoughts are entertained by the mind it will lead to the same actions. It is written in the Ivory Tablets of the Crow:

"*There is no sense of reasoning with these feelings. I have seen them possess the body of the unwary, causing fits of anger and all sorts of hypocrisies. And the power these feelings have over the body of man cannot be put into words. But when the spirit is* torn from the body these feelings act on their own accord and will haunt another house of flesh.

Know then that these feelings keep the spirit a prisoner in the house of flesh. They will make a blasphemy of the mind, so that the spirit becomes a worshipper of the same feelings that bind   him.

The Lakes of Shamhat

Shamhat is the first-begotten of the sorceresses that came to be known as the Jade Maidens. She is the door that opens the mind to other worlds, like the mouth of the body. Her domain is found in the Lakes of Nyarzir.

The Kiss of Shamhat is a pleasure that lasts for six days and seven nights. It was known in the times of remote antiquity that these six days were also the hexagram.

There are many who find comfort along the Lakes of Shamhat. It is a place of initiation, temples, and even baptism. The Lake's waters may be shallow at times and deep on other occasions. It is a symbol of the dream mind.

There is much refreshment near the Lake. It is place of peace and reflection. Shamhat is the first among the Jade Maidens to assist the Magician in the work of knowing. It is the energy of influence like the dream mind.

Shamhat reveals the place of residence of the true spirit and it will detect the words or thoughts and emotions that can either assist you in your work, or prevent you from understanding such.

There are many things that grow alongside the Lake enabling the magician to best understand voices of influence for positive and negative things, which take place between people.

Her sorcery can be found in words. The Magician knows that such things, including emotions and thoughts, are also actions that determine karma. It is a fertile place and these things do breed events that blossom.

Now the formula for entering the Lake of Shamhat is written here. The Opening of the Sea must occur, and the Soul of Fire Prayer and the Calling of the Shamuzi. These are the words and they must be recited thirteen times in front of the Wutzki:

Oot-eehzz-moo-ah-whoo-nn-bee, eek-hss-moo-ah-moo-ah-eehzz-oot, whoo-nn-bee-eehzz Shamhat!

Shamhat!

Oot-eehzz-moo-ah-whoo-nn-bee, eek-hss-moo-ah-moo-ah-eehzz-oot, whoo-nn-bee-eehzz Dui!

Dui!

After the Mountains of Xuz comes the Lakes of Shamhat. They are both of the same order, one full of vigor and the other receptive.

The Yi Jing Apocrypha of Genghis Khan

Shamhat is the young girl entering the age of knowing.
She is like the Moon and similar to water. The Lake,
however, is not the Moon, but the menstruating woman.
She is the Lake of menstrual blood. Remember, it is
written in the Ivory Tablets of the Crow:

*"The fiery ones, after seeing the motion of the Earth and the
recurrent destruction of man's civilizations, made an elixir to
preserve their offspring and the faithful priests and priestesses
who honored the sacred rites. The elixir is green in color and
somehow connected to the fruit of a woman during certain times
of the Moon."*

Seventeenth Hexagram

The Lake of Aozu

Sui

Priestess: Aozu

(Phe) Thunder in the Lake (Hmu) means that she will lead thee (Tuu) in the house of the mind.

The Seventeenth Letter of Genghis Khan to the Magicians of the Yi Jing:

Shamhat has called for many initiations, temples, and baptisms by the Lake. After the Magician has climbed the Mountain, he must follow the young girl and enter the place of knowing.

Indeed in each experience there is a place of beauty behind the veil. It is virtue that calls. The trail of blood is that of the Menstruating Woman. She is beautiful and pure, but cannot be touched during this time of the

Moon. It is for this reason that only those who are virtuous can follow her. Know that joy is her place of rest.

Twenty-Eighth Hexagram

The Lake of Asakhira

Da Guo

Priestess: Asakhira

(Aum) Lake calls the Wind. (Nzu) Some lower elements may whisper the blasphemies of negative deeds. (Bnhu) Stay on the path of goodness.

The Twenty-Eighth Letter of Genghis Khan to the Magicians of the Yi Jing:

When the Magician follows the Menstruating Woman, many people in the village will marvel at such a sight. Some will even inquire about the Magician's intentions, as it can be seen that they are not those associated with the lower passions. In spite of such, the Magician will stand firm against the public opinion.

This perspective is a necessary part of the sacred work. Generations will pass and few among the Common-folk will remember the stories of the Magician who followed the Menstruating Woman. Many are called to the sacred work in this manner.

When the spirit of the world is not centered on divine things, the Magician must live without regret. This is the lesson taught to him by the Menstruating Woman. He is not afraid to stand against the world.

During his climb up the Mountains, the Magician was approached by many people who put faith in the miraculous arts in order to solve their problems. However, the problems of the Common-folk are created by themselves for themselves. They only seek out the Magician as an easy answer to their problems. All gods are Magicians.

Many of these people were deceived by Fools who thought they were magicians, and the Common-folk believed in such. It is then that they meet and reject the Magician because his work is not like that of the Fool. It is true that the Magician must serve the sacred work. Yet, the Common-folk only seek to be surrounded by vanity. They are truly bound by the demons that enter their minds.

The Magician will turn away from such things without fear. He will continue to follow the Menstruating Woman, as she is without shame, an upright woman indee

Thirty-First Hexagram

The Lake of Zwa

Xian

Priestess: Zwa

(Aum) Keep an open mind (Aum) and safeguard virtue. (Hmu) People who are sincere will come to you.

The Thirty-First Letter of Genghis Khan to the Magicians of the Yi Jing:

The Magician will follow his true self. Although the Common-folk seek their own aims, the Magician must move humbly, never revealing the ailments incited by those who only seek their own glory. While acting in such a manner may seem vain for the Magician, he is trusted by the Menstruated Woman because of such.

For seven days and six nights, the Menstruating Woman and the Magician share in a deep and entwined passion.

The Yi Jing Apocrypha of Genghis Khan

The Magician marries the Menstruating Woman on the new moon. They both understand who they really are. Now they are who they really are.

Forty-Third Hexagram

The Lake of Chuki

Guai

Priestess: Chuki

(Zhee) Understanding has been revealed by the light. (Zhee) A decision must be made. (Phe) You must be determined and not waver because of negative surroundings.

The Forty-Third Letter of Genghis Khan to the Magicians of the Yi Jing:

If a teacher is truly sincere, he will teach his students a knowledge that will surpass his own. This is how his teachings are preserved for future generations.

The Menstruating Woman will teach the Magician knowledge through passion. Truth will always be truth.

The Yi Jing Apocrypha of Genghis Khan

There is nothing noble about truth. Truth can lie. It can hide the facts. The only truth that is good for use, is the truth that your emotional state creates your environment.

Give me passion, so I can understand how to shape the world. Give me a word of joy, so I can water my garden and make flowers grow. If you give me truth all I can do is argue with fools.

Forty-Fifth Hexagram

The Lake of Lalui

Cui

Priestess: Lalui

(Nzu) Wisdom begins with our ancestors. (Hmu) We can learn from their (Lewhu) wisdom. (Tuu) Sacrifice brings great success (Nzu) and true inner peace.

The Forty-Fifth Letter of Genghis Khan to the Magicians of the Yi Jing:

The Magician shall continue to seek the wisdom of his ancestors. He will appreciate such in sacrifice. The Magician's temple of sacrifice is his experience. The Menstruating woman is his temple.

Every month the Menstruating Woman provides a sacrifice for her ancestors, and in return she is provided with the ability to create life. Only that which can create life can offer sacrifice.

Forty-Seventh Hexagram

The Lake of Nhu

Kun

Priestess: Nhu

 (Shki) Difficulties solved, (Zhee) not by
words alone, but actions. (Bnhu) Oppression is a
discipline for success.

The Forty-Seventh Letter of Genghis Khan to the Magicians of the Yi Jing:

Words can please a woman, but the Menstruating
Woman is not pleased by words. The Magician will act
and fulfill the promises made by his word, success will
follow.

Whoever can control his words can control the weather.
Know that when the weather changes, new forces of
control are being appointed in government for the
benefit of the unseen lands.

108

Forty-Ninth Hexagram

The Lake of Burz

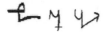

Ge

Priest: Burz

 (Hmu-Shki-Aum) Transformation. Remove useless sides of the persona

The Forty-Ninth Letter of Genghis Khan to the Magicians of the Yi Jing:

The Magician understands that the Menstruating Woman is in a state of constant renewal, which makes her a perfect replica of the universe.

Through the passion shared with the Menstruating Woman, the Magician understands the importance of shedding a side of himself with the changing seasons and knows the appropriate time to do so. Food eaten by its season is very beneficial. When food that is eaten in the wrong season it can kill you.

Fifty-Eighth Hexagram

The Lake of Shamhat

Dui

Ruler: Shamhat

(Bnhu) The call for the harvest, (Aum) yields a fine reward.

The Fifty-Eighth Letter of Genghis Khan to the Magicians of the Yi Jing:

The Lesson of the Menstruating Woman teaches the Magician that all that is within is without, and by the perseverance of virtue the Magician will remain in a harmonious state of immortality.

Many were called to the Art of Sacrifice, and all those who remembered such knew its origins came from the Menstruating Woman. In the case of the magician, it is not physical blood that must be shed, but a purification of the vital force.

Remember the voice of the Menstruating Woman, and the study thereof, is a key to many other workings. Know too, that the Lakes of Shamhat can be reached by the following formula:

Shamhat (3rd line)
Fahmu (2nd line)
Phe (1st line)

Now the first line of the trigram represents the Vasuh letter that must be vibrated along the Footprints of the Crow.

The second line of thee trigram is the formula, which must be enacted, for after words comes action. The third line is the place of entry is the sacred place of Nyarzir.

The Winds of Sheba

Sheba is the High Priestess of the Winds. She may be hard to perceive by some, but easily understood when one has traveled the journey. During the enjoyment of the Lakes of Shamhat, it is easy to look up and see the trees moving by the Hand of Sheba.

One cannot know the Way unless they know the Wind. Know that the Wind shapes the path. When the Winds are gentle, it is a time of pleasure for the Priest and Priestess, a measure to expand the work of benevolent forces. When the Winds are harsh and brutal it is for the purpose of guiding one to take a new course of action and a testimony of a new experience that is about to be born. These are the ways of the Winds of Sheba.

Remember that no god is the true god. The Wind is a great teacher of these things. It is the way of the Sorcerers since ancient times. She who can guide the Wind is truly a Sorceress. The Magician, when finding the Winds of Sheba, is no longer a Magician, but a Sorcerer or Sorceress.

The things in the place of Nyarzir are in all heavens and earths, but they are not to be worshipped. These things exist in the mind and in the heart of the Sorcerer, and by the invocation of such, the Sorcerer understands the work of Johuta the Mirror.

This knowledge has been set in motion so that the witnesses of certain phenomena can testify that there are indeed intelligences with their own mind and heart living alongside the race of man.

We invoke these things not out of fear and ignorance, but by the love that they have embraced us with in the material temple of the soul. It is with the acknowledgement of these very same natures that we cultivate the soul by returning what we have received.

The man, who does not embrace these natures, is living in a house without a home. This is the meaning of the journey and its course. The Winds of Sheba is the breeze that lifts the veil for all to see the glory of Nyarzir.

When the work of the Sorcerer and Sorceress is being prepared, the Winds of Sheba will come unto thee. Now the Opening of the Sea must occur, and the Soul of Fire Prayer and the Calling of the Shamuzi. These are the words and they must be recited four times in front of the Wutzki:

Whoo-nn-bee-eehzz, you-mmh-ha-eek-hss Sheba!

ᛞ ᛚᛟ , ᛖ ᛄ Sheba!
Whoo-nn-bee-eehzz, you-mmh-ha-eek-hss Xun!

ᛞ ᛚᛟ , ᛖ ᛄ ☵ Xun!

Always remember that after the Wutzki is called, in each and every working, the rites that preceded these and those after, the Sword of the Ninzuwu must be called and then one is prepared to use the formula:

114

Sheba (3rd line)
Iwuvh (2nd line)
Lewhu (1st line)

Ninth Hexagram

The Wind of Tasuta

Xiao Chu

Sorceress: Tasuta

(Hmu) Protect the eye from clouds that makes the soul weary, (Bnhu) blessings will surely follow.

The Ninth Letter of Genghis Khan to the magicians of the Yi Jing:

The Sorceress, when leaving the work of the Magician, must begin by exercising restraint. This work did apply for the Magician, but not in the midst of the same understanding. The Magician will invoke this and other things. The Sorcerer can read the signs of Heaven, understanding not only the logical meaning behind the experience, but the emotional cause behind such things.

116

The Wind among the small clouds that yield no rain
leads to a small harvest. When the Magician answers the
call of the Winds of Sheba and becomes a Sorcerer, he
must first rest from the passion shared with the
Menstruating Woman. He must spend time with himself
in order to renew his energy. An overabundance of
pleasure is an inseparable part of disease and sickness.

Twentieth Hexagram

The Wind of Kukunochi

Guan

Sorcerer: Kukunochi

(Hmu-Tuu) The temple is prepared when the mind is cleansed.

The Twentieth Letter of Genghis Khan to the Magicians of the Yi Jing:

Sorcery is an art of the Magician. Like the Wind, it is the knowing of the unseen cause producing the visible outcome. It is due to such, that this part of the journey is nothing more than a path of dreams. It is the path of the hunt.

In sorcery, one must cleanse the temple of the mind and heart in order to see the existing cause. Is it not like the

The Yi Jing Apocrypha of Genghis Khan

Wind? Remember how the great priest Xuz faired in the Wind. It is written in the Ivory Tablets of the Crow:

"*While walking through the mountains, he heard a great wind, but there was no breeze. He decided to climb a tree and wait. Some hours past, and when he was about to climb down from the tree, when he saw Johuta and Nudzuchi practicing the mysterious arts. On seeing these things Xuz revealed some of the customs and secrets of the fiery ones to his wife and daughter.*"

The Wind of Kukunochi is the great contemplation of thy destination. Before any act of sorcery, one must wash their hands. Know that man was created with two hands, one for the workings of Heaven, and the other for the workings of the Earth.

We wash our hands before any act of divination in order to clear the mind of otherworldly influences. This world now is divine. Time is an intricate form of imagination. However, the Sorcerer will displace himself from such things until the period of observation has transpired.

Thirty-Seventh Hexagram

The Wind of Ieh

Jia Ren

Sorceress: Ieh

(Zhee) Fire has breath in its life also. (Zhee) In this regard, we can say that some Winds are made of Fire. (Lewhu) These are the type that require perseverance and virtue.

The Thirty-Seventh Letter of Genghis Khan to the Magicians of the Yi Jing:

Once the hands have been cleansed, the powers of the Heavens and the Earth have been purified, fall into the place of the yin and focus on the breath of the fire. It is the Soul of Fire Prayer that has been preserved from a time before time. It is not the worship of gods, but the acknowledgement of a family that is often ignored by men. Although the Sorceress appears to live in two worlds, these worlds exist in the same place.

It is unfortunate that many of the Common-folk live in a world where they are not able to communicate with nature. The practitioner of the mysterious arts has a family that cannot be described in words literally. The fire is a cleansing force and a medium for our thoughts to travel to this family.

Forty-Second Hexagram

The Wind of Gzk

Yi

Sorcerer: Gzk

Zhee-Tuu-Hmu-Nzu-Aum means increase in Ninzuwu. (Zhee) Call upon the Soul of Fire in order to understand the light of the goddess. (Tuu) This will bring protect what has been cultivated (Hmu) and an increase in vitality. (Nzu) abundance will come in the preservation of these things. One must learn to project into the deeper spaces of the soul.

The Forty-Second Letter of Genghis Khan to the Magicians of the Yi Jing:

The Sorcerer will set his destination upon the dream plane and gather what he can for the sake of his family and for his survival.

He will cross the river only to demonstrate the cause of what appears in this world. The Wind of Gzk stands over Thunder and shapes the voice of destiny.

Cultivation of such things is a necessary step in preserving our sacred tradition. Stay with this course and disregard the unnecessary things. No mother will allow a baby to sit in its own wastes.

It is an art that can only be preserved with clarity of mind, and clinging to what is pure. Know that the Common-folk are weighed down by unclean things. Immortality is preserved in the body of man, but many forfeit this gift for the demons that plague the soul. Guard against these things.

Know that what is impure, in the sacred work of thy soul, fortifies the wall between this place of phenomena and its invisible cause. It is written in the Ivory Tablets of the Crow:

"*Beyond the stars, beyond the darkness of the night they dwell. Into the realm of light they reside in stillness. Without need of the elements, for what is it? It is consciousness. The mere reflection of this statement caused that which is self-aware to stare at itself in darkness. Yet, it remains whole.*"

Fifty-Third Hexagram

The Wind of Jhn

Jian

Sorceress: Jhn

(Zhee) The fire of the goddess is useful and can never overcook (Bnhu) what is nourishing.

The Fifty-Third Letter of Genghis Khan to the Magicians of the Yi Jing:

The Sorceress begins the journey. It is a marriage for some. It was at one time a course of the true lords, those of legend who would step over the river and marry a worthy bride. These things still take place in this era, here and now. There were many brides who crossed the river only to bring the technologies of the unveiled into this form and fashion.

The Yi Jing Apocrypha of Genghis Khan

It is also known that there were many men, vested in the magical arts, who walked with an unseen bride. Indeed, there will come a time when the Alchemical Man must pass from this realm and the offspring that he produced with the unseen bride will come to his aid. Until this time, be satisfied with the harvest from the radiant dream.

Fifty-Seventh Hexagram

The Wind of Sheba

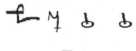

Xun

Ruler: Sheba

 (Hmu) Desire is the first
Wind, (Shki) then it dies and is buried in some thought.
(Bnhu) Plants grow in the same manner. There is small
success ahead.

The Fifty-Seventh Letter of Genghis Khan to the Magicians of the Yi Jing:

Before the Sorceress enters the dream world, she must
find an anchor in the dream realm. The mind must let
the Wind carry their consciousness to the appropriate
place. Impure thoughts are not allowed in these spaces
and such will draw one back to this world. The Wind
must straddle the Wind, one thought in one location.

The Great Man must be met along the way. He is the inspector of thoughts and desires, but there is no worry over such things. The Wind must straddle the Wind, one thought for each location.

Fifty-Ninth Hexagram

The Wind of Lzwa

Huan

Sorceress: Lzwa

Success is born after the call of the ancestors is made.

The Fifty-Ninth Letter of Genghis Khan to the Magicians of the Yi Jing:

The "gods" live in the subconscious, but our ancestors survive in our blood. Our work is to set aside the ego and discover the hidden potential buried deep in the Kunlun Mountains. This process is eternal.

Men study the changes, but the Magicians of the Yi Jing use the hexagrams to create changes. Slaves are subjects not of kings, but changes. There are things more powerful than the Sun and Moon. These things must be respected also.

128

In humility, we are reminded of those that preceded us on the path. Their wisdom is wise and their courage is strong.

Sixty-First Hexagram

The Wind of Kuhvi

لسل لسل

Zhong Fu

Sorceress: Kuhvi

لسل لسل (Phe) Allow the inner truth to (Phe) judge the inner truth in others.

The Sixty-First Letter of Genghis Khan to the Magicians of the Yi Jing:

Returning from the ancestral temple, we see the reflection of the ancestor gods in us. Our behavior is founded on such relations. Remember, that our enemies are enslaved by these influences. Those who hold the unseen power of life and death were given the blessing of radiance for fair judgment.

The Common-folk have families too. They may be our enemy, but they are loved by others, their family. It is proper to measure the rite of magic and how its sum will fit into the movements of the Heaven. Remember, they

are subjects of the heavenly way of things. The exception
for the practitioner of the mysterious arts, does not
afford one the ability to avoid the decrees of heaven, but
the opportunity to turn what is given from the stars into
a nourishing substance for the soul. The Common-folk
receive the same portion, but allow their lower passions
to consume what was rightfully theirs. Do not let
yourself be a victim of your own needs. Act with virtue
and honor.

The Wind of Kuhvi is the teacher of truth and lies.
Many claim to know truth, but only seek to confirm a
history, which is no more than an opinion of an
experience. It is a treasure only sought after by Fools.
They cannot see that their "truth" is nothing more than a
lie.

Remember this lesson well and let it guide you through
the course of your work. The truth of the mysterious arts
is not found in the testimony of an experience or the
validity of its existence. Nor is it an analysis of some
event. This is the way of Fools.

A lie is when a Fool relates an account in history that
did exist, but the discussion over these things produces a
bad emotion in the man who listens to such. This is the
lie. The Fool has two tongues, for he speaks accurately of
a history, but the meaning of such speeches brings a dark
cloud into the heart of the listener, even though the
history being taught by the Fool did occur. This is a lie,
for it has bred an evil emotion in the heart of the
listener. And the Fool will continue to promote his truth
as a truth among the Common-folk who will accept it as
such. The truth of the Fool is a lie in the Court of
Heaven and a means of spiritual attack on the unwary.

Before you cast judgment upon others, think about your
own thoughts and desires that have lied to you in this
same fashion.

The truth that can be known is not the truth. The truth is a process that nourishes the soul and is a different way for each and every individual who knows the way. The truth will not produce a debate over recorded histories, but helps the sincere seeker see the cause that created such histories.

Still the Fool is unaware of the unseen cause that moves behind all things, existing outside the walls of time. Man is time moving in a straight line with the Heavens and Earth above him. He was fashioned as the result, but his purpose is to become the cause. It is for this reason that in the days of remote antiquity women were honored as such.

It was the Wu who created the Way. The Way that is studied cannot be understood until Wu comes to thee as a teacher of the Way. The Way exists only in the womb of the Great Mother. It is written in the Ivory Tablets of the Crow:

"*It is during the Baptism of the Ancient One that the Goddess revives the spirit. It is like a child being born into this world. When the child is in the womb, it is in this world, but it is in the mother's body. When the child is born it must know how to take care of itself.*"

This Book of Changes is nothing more than a calendar of birth for the unborn. The secret of the Sorceress comes in knowing that intercourse is the cause for all things coming and going, passing from one womb to the next. Even man's ability to generate semen was created in the womb.

What more is there after the Sorceress? Surely, she knows the Art of the Womb. Prepare for the spirit of another nature.

The Thunder of Yuvho

Yuvho is the Thunder of Nyarzir and entrance into the innermost part of the mind of the Magician. It is not a place of ritual, but of spirit. The Thunders of Yuvho is a swift moving force. His smile is the strike of lightning when the sun has reached the heights of heaven. It is written in the Ivory Tablets of the Crow:

"But Yuvho saw the brightness of the Earth and took up residence in its Sun. Later, he constructed Seven Gardens on Earth, each resembling a city that exits inside the world that stands outside of time. The Army of Yuvho descended upon the Earth in Seven Dreams, Shamuzi being the first among them."

The Thunder of Yuvho is a vehicle of spirit behind the initial cause created in Heaven. It is not a place of ritual, but ritual can be performed until the spirit can walk. It is a rite not connected in flesh though it can be seen from the material eye.

Now the formula for intercourse with the Thunder of Yuvho is performed in the spirit. One must know that the spirit is not the dream, but dreams are within the spirit and Thunder and Lightning is the presence of an obscure phenomena pertaining to such. If it can be explained it can be manipulated. However, the workings of the innermost mind do not fall under this sort of jurisdiction.

Know the training of this course must come with what can be held on to in the deeper part of the mind. It is in the chamber of imagination that one can receive the blessings of Yuvho.

Now the Opening of the Sea must occur. The Soul of Fire prayer must be engaged, and the Calling of the Shamuzi will then follow. Afterwards, call Wutzki and the Ninzuwu.

When all of these operations have been performed, set thy mind upon an image of lightning and thunder in the face of the sun. You will be called in front of the Faceless One. When these things have occurred recite the following:

Yuvho eehzz-oot-moo-ah-eek-hss! Yuvho moo-ah-eek-hss-whoo-nn-bee-moo-ah!
Yuvho

Moo-ah-moo-ah-eek-hss-you-mmh-ha-eh-ph Zhen, ooh-wel-whoo-nn-bee-moo-ah Zhen,

This formula must be recited three times after one has secured the necessary steps. This is the formula for the trigram:

Yuvho (3rd line)
Zasosu (2nd line)
Tuu (1st line)

Now the language of these words is preserved in the smallest particle of the universe and in the massive array of stars. Use the mind that you have created in order to witness the brilliant Thunders of Yuvho.

Sixteenth Hexagram

The Thunder of Iut

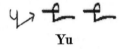

Yu

Emperor: Iut

 (Aum) When the soul begins to awaken, (Hmu) there is a bright emanation of appreciation and loving energy. (Hmu) This is Thunder over the Earth and the joy experienced because of such is the result of proper cultivation of the sexual energies.

The Sixteenth Letter of Genghis Khan to the Magicians of the Yi Jing:

The divine realm should not be mistaken for the ghostly world. The distinction between the two will be remembered by your soul.

The glory of the divine realm is a place drenched in abundance of harmony and melody. The voice of true prayer is always the work of a sacred musical instrument. Music is the first Thunder.

The Fool will pray in a tone that is not harmonious and not melodious. His prayers are heard by the ghostly spirits of that realm. They are attracted to such sounds, as they are similar to the noises heard deep within the Earth. Heaven, however, is reached by the beautiful language of song. All prayers of Heaven are songs composed by the birds in preparation of inhabiting a human body.

The Soul of Fire prayer is a beautiful song when spoken correctly. The Art of Prayer is only known to a few. It appears to the Common-folk as worship, but it is the practice of moving, receiving, and sending energy within this space in time and to places where time does not exist.

There are many people who pray in temples, but may not know the true meaning of prayer. The prayers said in temples are like the crumbs of bread left in a beggar's cup. Praying in temples is a useful exercise, but such is not the case in Heaven. It's like the soldier training for the battle. Once the battle begins, the soldier's training is over. It is the same with prayer.

Our prayers are our thoughts and feelings. This is the true meaning of any prayer or incantation. The prayers said in temples are exercises for the mind. It is nothing more than the practice of getting the mind to focus on a beneficent thought or feeling for a certain amount of time. This is a practice of mental endurance, not prayer. Once we leave the temple, our prayer begins and is found in our thoughts and feelings. Prayer is a magical act. Remember what is written in the Ivory Tablets of the Crow:

"Know then that these feelings keep the spirit a prisoner in the house of flesh. They will make a blasphemy of the mind, so that

the spirit becomes a worshipper of the same feelings that bind him. They often change into the shapes of gods and make the mind its disciple. There are also the feelings that inspire men. These too act as his gods. They seek to free the spirit from its slavery, but it is confused because the mind worships a false god.

Know that the Workers of the Miraculous Arts in the world before saw these things in parable, and gave each feeling a name, thereby binding it to a particular function. It was then that the spirit was free to rise up back to its throne again."

Thirty-Second Hexagram

The Thunder of Aeuq

Heng

Emperor: Aeuq

(Tuu) Our integrity begins with (Aum) what we have to say to ourselves and others.

The Thirty-Second Letter of Genghis Khan to the Magicians of the Yi Jing:

Know that the Emperor has a fixed course that is consistent with the times. There is much success in pursuit of such. It is so beautiful that it becomes mechanical, and so mechanical that it becomes perfect. It becomes so perfect that it begins to die. All mechanisms eventually pass away in this manner, but the Emperor is immortal.

I know it is not easy to understand, as these things did not come about by themselves. Coincidence is not a choice of the Magician, but a gate on the path. In the same manner, the Emperor is not the shell. Accordingly, we read of such in the Ivory Tablets of the Crow:

"Know that the Workers of the Miraculous Arts in the world before saw these things in parable, and gave each feeling a name, thereby binding it to a particular function. It was then that the spirit was free to rise up back to its throne again."

And the Common-folk cannot understand the Emperor. They laugh at those who worship an Emperor, but they themselves worship an unseen god. They themselves worship an existing authority while resenting the nation of their birth and pay tribute to such. However, the Magician has made his choice and will continue to worship the sovereign powers inside his own being while respecting those that sit on thrones. The Ninzuwu are Emperors of their own accord.

Let it be known, that if there is one worthy Magician of the Yi Jing living among you, then that place will prosper. These things were written during the days of old, the Emperor said:

"When a sage Ruler appears in the world and rules the Empire, Heaven is responsive to him, and manifests favorable omens. In this our Land of Japan, during the reign of the Emperor Homuda,'" a white crow made its nest in the Palace. In the time of the Emperor Ohosazaki, a Dragon-horse appeared in the West.'" This shows that from ancient times until now, there have been many cases of auspicious omens appearing in response to virtuous rulers. What we call phoenixes, unicorns, white pheasants, white crows, and such like birds and beasts, even including herbs and trees, in short all things having the property of significant response, are favorable omens and auspicious signs produced by Heaven and Earth.

Now that wise and enlightened sovereigns should obtain such auspicious omens is meet and proper. But why should We, who are so empty and shallow, have this good fortune? It is no doubt wholly due to our Assistants, the Ministers, Omi, Muraji, Tomo no Miyakko and Kuni no Miyakko, each of whom, with the utmost loyalty, conforms to the regulations that are made. For this reason, let all, from the Ministers down to the functionaries ' with pure hearts reverence the gods of Heaven and Earth, and one and all accepting the glad omen, make the Empire to flourish."

Thirty-Fourth Hexagram

The Thunder of Jimmu

Da Zhuang

Emperor: Jimmu

(Tuu) The Emperor follows the Way of Heaven, as it is the Path of Great Power. Thunder in Heaven, the voice of the Soul of Fire prayer, is an initiation of the stars.

The Thirty-Fourth Letter of Genghis Khan to the Magicians of the Yi Jing:

The Fool thinks that power can be obtained by means of some action or treaty. There is no power in such things. Remember that power is often confused with greed. The influence of greed only attracts greed, but in the eyes of the Common-folk it appears as power.

In order to gain power, one must follow the ways of Heaven and Earth. One must study the nature of the cosmic forces that influence men so as to know the ruling emotion of the moment. This is the beginning of choice and there is no power without choice. And the choices we make can only be borrowed from Heaven and Earth. We can make no choice on our own. Every opportunity is borrowed from Heaven and Earth. Every god that has condemned his servant to death, due to his human nature, is a demon. Nobody owns the land. Power is a borrowed opportunity from Heaven. Where there is life, there is power.

This is how the Emperor is able to discern greed from power. Power is a choice and a choice is an opportunity borrowed from Heaven and Earth. The Emperor knows that his kingdom is only the result of a fate that transpired between Heaven and Earth. It is written concerning Emperor Jimmu:

"Then Amaterasu no Obo-kami instructed the Emperor in a dream of the night, saying: "I will now send thee the Yatagarasu," make it thy guide through the land." Then there did indeed appear the Yatagarasu flying down from the Void. The Emperor said: " The coming of this crow is in due accordance with my auspicious dream. How grand! How splendid! My Imperial ancestor, Amaterasu no Ohkami, desires therewith to assist me in creating the hereditary institution."

Fortieth Hexagram

The Thunder of Wosado

Xie

Emperor: Wosado

(Aum) The Emperor knows the laws of nature (Tuu), or has at least (Tuu) studied them. (Phe) Nature forgives and rules in (Bnhu) fairness as does the Emperor.

The Fortieth Letter of Genghis Khan to the Magicians of the Yi Jing:

Who can escape the law of karma? Still you ponder over such questions, but the answer is quite simple. Forgiveness is the greatest power in the world. Yet, the Common-folk believe that death is the payment for sin. The power of forgiveness is greater than the power of god. Things of this sort are the work of wicked voices in the night. Death is change. It can never be used as a form of payment unless it is offered to animal spirits and deceptive natures.

It is easy for one to reconcile the error of their ways. Forgiveness and repentance is the greatest power in the world. When the Emperor exercises forgiveness and repentance and encourages such among his subjects, his kingdom will flourish.

Fifty-First Hexagram

The Thunder of Yuvho

Zhen

Ruler: Yuvho

(Zhee) The light of the goddess can take any shape, (Tuu) even that of Thunder. (Aum) The Emperor who has access to such forces must also respect the sacred art (Shki) in reverential fear, knowing that he exercises the will of Heaven and Earth while occupying the body of man.

The Fifty-First Letter of Genghis Khan to the Magicians of the Yi Jing:

There is no decree that can be made in the Emperor's kingdom that was not pronounced by the will of Heaven and Earth. Those who study the stars know the truth of this matter very well.

146

The Yi Jing Apocrypha of Genghis Khan

The Emperor must act in accord with the will of Heaven and Earth. Know that the fear of the Emperor is a different fear than the Common-folk.

The Common-folk live in fear of their lives, not knowing the end result of death. The Emperor lives in fear of not acting in accord with the ways of Heaven, knowing that his retribution is the fate of his descendants after his death.

Fifty-Fourth Hexagram

The Thunder of Viyah

(handwritten glyphs)

Gui Mei

Empress: Viyah

(handwritten glyphs) (Zhee) The Emperor who has been (Lewhu) initiated into the ways of the Ninzuwu (Aum) must count his actions today (Zhee) as the fate of his (Zhee) future tomorrow. Thunder over the Lake is a sign that the youngest daughter will marry before the eldest one.

The Fifty-Fourth Letter of Genghis Khan to the Magicians of the Yi Jing:

When it is time for the Emperor to marry, he must be aware of the result of his actions, always keeping the fates of Heaven and Earth in thy heart. Every action has some result in the future. Be cautious and do not give way to presumptuous actions. It is customary to marry the eldest daughter first. However, it is not for the pressing desires that the Emperor engages in marriage, for he knows that a divine heir can only be produced by the aid of a High Priestess.

The Common-folk will simply marry out of desire. These are the same desires that keep men in chains. The decisions that they make can be found in the faith they hold in the god of chance. They have been misled into believing that civilization changes with the times. They are truly misled. It has been known from the ages of old that there is nothing new under the Sun. They cannot see that the youngest daughter held the eldest daughter as the principle of womanhood.

Their misconception is like that of a young child, every new invention is a new embrace that captivates the imagination. Men build machines. The machines are changing, but man is still the same. Men believe in gods. The gods are evolving, but man is still the same. However, the practice of virtue makes way for the pleasure of the young maiden in old age. It is written in the Ivory Tablets of the Crow:

"*After the last destruction, Yuvho created a fine image of man to inhabit during his visit to Earth. He gave instructions to the Yuvhoa and the Zhee to ensure the restoration of man's civilizations and withdrew the Difu from the world that exists in time. It was during this time that his passion was aroused by the Goddess Viyah. Yuvho employed a mortal king to build a temple for Viyah and himself, called Ioxna. Afterwards, he administered tasks to the Zhee, concerning Muh.*"

Many read these words and still do not understand. They will question the Emperor about his marriage to the young maiden, thinking that it will lead to misfortune as it is not the custom for those of the East. It is true that there is nothing new under the Sun.

Fools they are! They forget that the Emperor is a
Magician and that the young maiden is the Lake of
Shamhat. There is nothing new under the Sun, but the
Way of Knowing is hidden from the sight of the
Common-folk. It is written in the Ivory Tablets of the
Crow:

*"Yuvho created a fine image of man to inhabit during his visit to
Earth. He gave instructions to the Yuvhoa and the Zhee to
ensure the restoration of man's civilizations and withdrew the
Difu from the world that exists in time. It was during this time
that his passion was aroused by the Goddess Viyah."*

The Emperor has married the young maiden since the
days of antiquity, for there is a knowledge in the passion
of Shamhat that is unearthly nature. If this knowledge
is procured with intelligence and virtue, it will unlock
the gate of the unseen cause. This was known since the
beginning of the world. It was written during the Age of
the Gods:

**"Izanagi no Mikoto, wishing to see his younger sister,
went to the Netherworld. At this time, Izanami no
Mikoto being still as she was when alive came forth to
meet him. She spoke to Izanagi no Mikoto and said, 'My
husband, I beseech thee not to look upon me.' When she
was done speaking, she became invisible. It was then
dark, so Izanagi no Mikoto lit a single light, and looked
upon her. Izanami no Mikoto was swollen and festering,
and eight kinds of Thunder-Gods rested upon her.
Izanagi no Mikoto was shocked and fled. The Thunder-
Gods chased him.**

**Now by the roadside there grew a large peach tree, at the
foot of which Izanagi no Mikoto hid himself. He took
the fruit of the peach tree and hurled it at the Thunder-
Gods and the Thunder Gods ran away. This was the
origin of the practice of keeping evil spirits away by
means of the peach tree and its fruit. Then Izanagi flung**

down his staff, saying: 'The thunders may not come beyond this.' The staff was called Funado no Kami, and was originally called Kunado no Ohoji.

Of the so-called Eight Thunders, that which was on her head was called the Great Thunder; that which was on her breast was called the Fire-Thunder; that which was on her belly was called the Earth-Thunder; that which was on her back was called the Young-Thunder; that which was on her posteriors was called the Black-Thunder; that which was on her hand was called Mountain-Thunder; that which was on her foot was called the Moor-Thunder; and that which was on her genitals was called the Cleaving-Thunder."

The Emperor knows that the technology of the Eight Thunders is obtained by intercourse with the young maiden, also known as the High Priestess. Yet, the Emperor, like Izanagi-no-Mikoto, is in possession of a staff whereby these powers can be cultivated for safety of his kingdom. It is written in the Ivory Tablets of the Crow:

"*Stay with the Soul of Fire*
It is a Prayer of Fire that has been preserved
From a time that was before time

It is the Power of Lightening
Crooked in its shape
It is the Prayer of Fire

The Prayer of Fire
Is the glance
When that which is Self-Aware
Stares at itself"

Fifty-Fifth Hexagram

The Thunder of Malukedek

Feng

Emperor: Malukedek

(Aum) The one who invokes Heaven (Lewhu) can give good judgment among men. The brilliance of his conduct is a refreshment among the nations.

The Fifty-Fifth Letter of Genghis Khan to the Magicians of the Yi Jing:

The Emperor will follow the ways of Heaven and Earth. He has embraced the world of immortality, He does not look upon favoritism and pride to fulfill his obligations.

The Emperor knows that the way of Heaven and Earth is the way of Man and Woman. The nations of antiquity prospered for this very same reasons. It is written in the Ivory Tablets of the Crow:

"And Mezek grew in wisdom and conquered many lands. He was a renowned one among the generations of men and found favor in the eyes of the gods. He taught the rites of the sacred fruit found in the pleasure of women. He is known to some as Malukedek."

Sixty-Second Hexagram

The Thunder of Raijin

Xiao Guo

Emperor: Sugawara no Michizane

(Phe) A concern for others is useful in obtaining small rewards. (Aum) Remain in virtue throughout the discourse of harmony. Doubt breeds doubt.

The Sixty-Second Letter of Genghis Khan to the Magicians of the Yi Jing:

If the Emperor does not remember himself on every occasion, he will fall victim to excessive grieving. Excessive indulgence in small things brings about small rewards. Doubt is the first sign of an evil spirit in thy presence. It is written in the Ivory Tablets of the Crow:

"It was then that man turned away from his true spirit. The feelings that once served man began to rise in power. Over time

the spirit of man became enslaved to his feelings once again. Many lives were lost as the powers of the feelings over men began to grow. Man's history became filled with bloodshed and things loathsome to the flesh, causing a great noise.

The Ninzuwu heard the noise of pain and sorrow. They remembered the Oracle of Man and saw all the spirits that were held in bondage.

The Ninzuwu called their Children. The Ninzuwu sent dreams to awaken their Children. Now many of the Children saw the dream, but did not remember the formula. They wrote about such things in their Books of Fables. Among these Children the formula appeared as something connected with the dead."

The Flames of Amaterasu

Amaterasu-Omikami is the Woman of the Sun, also known as Wutzki. No evil can stand in the presence of Amaterasu-Omikami, Where there is Fire, there is no shadow or shade.

The knowledge of Amaterasu-Omikami is obscure indeed. Her presence was found in Heaven and Earth before she was even born. There is Fire in the Earth and there is Fire in Heaven.

There are others who accused Amaterasu of being of the race of the Ayaqox, as she is able to hold intercourse with many elements, and Fire is created by rubbing two rocks together. Yet, the Mystery of Amaterasu is a testimony for all to see her fragrance of light in every part of creation.

Amaterasu (3rd line)
Dehfu (2nd line)
Aum (12st line)

Now the Call of Amaterasu is given later in this writing, but it must be used to open the Heavenly Gate after the Initiation of the Crow. Amaterasu is the protective force for those entering the Waters. The preliminary steps are of a different order.

Now the Opening of the Sea must take place, the Soul of Fire and the Calling of the Shamuzi invoked. Afterwards, call upon the Ninzuwu. Now the image of Amaterasu, the Woman of Fire, must be kept in the mind's eye while reciting these words three times:

Amaterasu moo-ah-eehzz=moo-ah! Ooh-zz-nn-eehzz-ooh-zz-nn, eek-hss-eehzz-eh-ph, moo-ah-moo-ah-eh-ph-you-mmh-ha Amaterasu!

Amaterasu

Those who know the Mystery of Amaterasu are certain that she is the Fire that moves through the body. It is for this reason that she must be called with the formula given later in this writing.

Fourteenth Hexagram

The Flame of Hahun

Da You

Prophet: Hahun

(Zhee) In spirit (Bnhu) there is wealth. In spirit there is joy in living.

The Fourteenth Letter of Genghis Khan to the Magicians of the Yi Jing:

The Fool that is rich can never be wealthy. Many are deceived by rich Fools. Wealth can only be acquired by virtue. Virtue suppresses evil.

Surely, I have seen the misfortune that befalls a whole nation. There are many rich people living in poverty. Some are planning a revolt in an attempt to regain power. They are Fools! Heaven has decreed the proper fate for them.

The only way an impoverished people can become wealthy is through acts of virtue. It they have not devised a plan that will improve the world that they are living in, then they are not worthy to rule the world and will never find wealth. The wealthy man will not follow the footsteps of a rich man. The wealthy man seeks to fulfill the will of Heaven and Earth.

The rich man is evil, as he only seeks to enjoy the pleasures of the flesh. His evil is a result of his ignorance. The Fool does not know the meaning of life. When some sage or prophet advises him about the meaning of life, he will call it the work of evil spirits. The Fool is under the influence of demons. He will only use what he has gained to impress others and seek their admiration instead of turning their attention towards the way of Heaven and Earth. It is for this reason that the Fool, who is rich, will always be poor and a curse to his ancestors.

Take up the ways of virtue and remain armed against the evil forces. Know that the experience of wickedness is a painful lover that prevents the beneficial fate. Remember the Soul of Fire prayer. It is a lesson for those who are in the Mind of Heaven. It is written in the Ivory Tablets of the Crow:

"It is said that the name of this place is called Vasuh and Ut, the twin cities of water and fire, recorded in the histories of men, as the Tree of Life. The children of the fiery ones are called Hahun,"

Twenty-First Hexagram

The Flame of Shapash

Shi Ke

Prophetess: Shapeash

 (Phe) Awareness of one's emotions
(Aum) is a necessary part of understanding (Nzu) true
morality.

The Twenty-First Letter of Genghis Khan to the
Magicians of the Yi Jing:

Before the Prophetess pursues the way of Heaven and
Earth, she must begin setting up the boundaries of her
practice. This is true for every aspect of her life, for they
are all really only one aspect.

Honesty is required in the course of such things. In the
beginning, the student is without clarity, unaware of

certain unseen laws. Such a woman is not in the condition to negotiate boundaries, but she can commit to being in an honest relationship with her lover, or her teacher. Success always follows honesty. A dishonest person has made chaos out of the simple things in life.

Thirtieth Hexagram

The Flame of Amaterasu-Omikami

Li

Ruler: Amaterasu-Omikami

(Zhee) The brilliance of the Lady of Heaven (Lewhu) shines forth in those who follow the ways of Heaven and Earth.

The Thirtieth Letter of Genghis Khan to the Magicians of the Yi Jing:

Know that the foundation of the Art of Ninzuwu is in the cultivation of the Fire of the Sun and Moon. These are the first of many teachers that the Prophet will encounter from birth. The Fool will ignore such phenomena and believe that these things have come by chance. Yet in still, the physicians of the civilized nations know that the luminaries in Heaven cause changes in the body. Is this not a law also?

Know that since the beginning the course of the brilliance in Heaven is perfect. When the brilliance of our internal sun reaches that which is in Heaven, the *reikon will live in accord with the four souls*. Does not the Bride of Nyarzir have four faces? These, and other Mysteries of the Heavenly Lady, have meaning as to how the hexagrams were created. It is written concerning the Age of the Gods:

"After this Izanagi no Mikoto and Izanami no Mikoto consulted each other, saying: "We have produced the Great eight-island country, with the mountains, rivers, herbs and trees. Why should we not produce someone who shall be lord of the universe? Afterwards, they produced the Sun-Goddess, who is called Amaterasu-no-Okami.

The brilliance of this child shone throughout all *six quarters*. Izanagi no Mikoto and Izanami no Mikoto rejoiced saying: we have had many children, but none of them have been equal to the wondrous infant. She ought not to be kept long in this land, but we ought of our own accord to send her at once to Heaven, and entrust her the affairs of Heaven."

During this time, Heaven and Earth were still not far separated, and therefore they sent her up to Heaven by the ladder of Heaven."

The movements of the Sun in Heaven are the lessons of the Sages. The Sun's ascent up the Heavenly ladder is a book full of wisdom and a primary law in this universe.

When the Prophet inculcates the Law of the Sun into his very being, by studying the Art of Ninzuwu, he will becomes like the Sun itself and a creature of nature that can impart life to others. It is written in the Ivory Tablets of the Crow:

"And the Cup of Fahmu can be filled with the Immortal Fire anytime one pleases, but best to do so before one sleeps. Once filled, it can be used during the Day of an Endless Age. The formulae is not a difficult task, save to push the air, containing

the fire, out of the body while one whispers 〰 ."

Thirty-Fifth Hexagram

The Flame of Nuru

ᛒ

Jin

Prophetess: Nuru

ᛒ (Bnhu) Progress and the dawning of
consciousness are a part of dreaming.

The Thirty-Fifth Letter of Genghis Khan to the Magicians of the Yi Jing:

Every new day is welcomed by the laughter of birds.
When the Sun is over the Earth, new things begin. The
Prophetess, keeping the ways of Heaven and Earth, must
awaken before the dawn and pay respect to her ancestor.

In ancient times, it was known that the gathering of
emotions can cause changes in the weather. Men built
kingdoms behind this science. They propagated religion
to ensure good weather for a fruitful harvest. It is
written in the Ivory Tablets of the Crow:

"*The fiery ones, after seeing the motion of the Earth and the recurrent destruction of man's civilizations, made an elixir to preserve their offspring and the faithful priests and priestesses who honored the sacred rites.*"

Thirty-Eighth Hexagram

The Flame of Yu Niu

Kui

Prophetess: Yu Niu

(Phe) There is unity (Aum) despite the diversity among those living in the village. (Shki) The Prophetess is praised as holy due to her nudity.

The Thirty-Eighth Letter of Genghis Khan to the Magicians of the Yi Jing:

Nudity is without blame. The Prophetess can hear the voice of Heaven and Earth in her nudity. She can give birth in the nakedness of her heart.

Now the Prophetess is aware of her nakedness while standing in the midst of the Common-folk. And the Common-folk are drawn to the wisdom of the Prophetess, but cannot see her nakedness. The nakedness of the Prophetess is found in the brilliance of her aura, and this has been known since times of remote antiquity. When one can see the nakedness of another, it was sign that they are trying to take the vital energy from the deepest part of the unseen temple.

Fiftieth Hexagram

The Flame of Kagutsuchi

Ding

Cauldron: Kagutsuchi

(Hmu) The work of the Cauldron is cherished in the Way of the Gods. It is the vessel of the correct path. Success will follow those who invoke the Cauldron. (Hmu) The Cauldron is an expression of a pure heart and an instrument used to secure thy position in Heaven.

The Fiftieth Letter of Genghis Khan to the Magicians of the Yi Jing:

The History of the Cauldron is the Way of the Gods. It is a symbol of Fire over Wind, and the meaning of this is obscure, but Fire must breathe also. The Prophetess knows the Ways of the Wind and Fire and how to plant the seeds of Fire upon the surface of the Wind. These secrets are known to those who have witnessed the birth of the Cauldron.

Now the Cauldron is born out of lust by a daughter of the Netherworld. It is a symbol of the Sun's ability to pronounce judgments during its course through the Underworld, a purifier of the hidden mind. An uncultivated Fire can run wild, like the fire in the wind. But the Ninzuwu can shape the Wind into a vessel that can contain the Fire by the use of the sacred language. It is written in the Ivory Tablets of the Crow:

"The reciting of Lustful Words must occur for Seven Days upon which no desirous contact can be made. After the Seven Days have passed, Ayaqox will visit thee in a dream and give unto you The Stone Bowl of Eternity.

When you receive the Stone Bowl in the Dream, you must fashion one like it upon awakening. And the Stone Bowl has many secrets, but it must be written about elsewhere, save that it must be made large enough to hold the Fire that one must pray over. When the Dream has ended, Ayaqox will reveal the Door of the Pure Place to you."

The words spoken over the Cauldron are like the Wind, but the heart is the Fire that stands over it. It is by use of this formula that many wondrous things come into being. And the Wind will carry the Fire of one's heart to the appropriate place in Heaven. Thereafter, an experience is born that bears the testimony of this work. These things were written about during the Age of the Gods concerning Kagutsuchi.

Fifty-Sixth Hexagram

The Flame of Fujiyama

Lu

Prophetess: Fujiyama

(Bnhu) Good fortune will arrive (Phe) is small ways. Let those that wander upon the path seek goodness.

The Fifty-Sixth Letter of Genghis Khan to the Magicians of the Yi Jing:

The thoughts that we carry in our minds are the steps we create in order to reach our aspirations. Exercise caution in the actions of the mind.

Our thoughts are judged by Heaven and Earth. Still you do not understand. Is not Heaven and Earth a part of our internal being? Fools speak about these things, but misinterpret the meaning, thinking with their conscious minds, they put faith in the servant and not the master.

The Fool has heard that magical powers are all part of his mind. Mistakenly, he then attempts to use his conscious mind to control the unseen aspects of life. The Fool has put faith in the servant rather than the master.

Be cautious in thy undertakings in all chambers of life, making sure the way of Heaven and Earth is thy course.

Sixty-Fourth Hexagram

The Flame of Tengu

Ƭo ᵻ∨ Ƭo ₤

Wei Ji

Prophet: Tengu

Ƭo ᵻ∨ Ƭo ₤ (Zhee) Fire over (Tuu) Water.
(Zhee) The Prophet understands that the journey is not
complete. A Prophet is not the end of the journey for
there are hidden treasures in the depth of the sea, though
forbidding. Use of discernment is an accessory in finding
success.

The Sixty-Fourth letter of Genghis Khan to the Magicians of the Yi Jing:

The Prophet is not the end of the journey, but has taken
the wise course, as he is armed with Fire. A Prophet is a
Prophet, but the arts of immortality are not the way of
the prophet in itself. One step on the journey is not the
journey itself.

The Art of Ninzuwu is the Art of Fire and Water. It is
written in the Ivory Tablets of the Crow:

*"Know that all things exist in water, and that water is the space
that the Dream exists in. Fire is the power that radiates its
influence over the Dream, and the ancients would create "gods"
out of those that shine the brightest."*

The Waters of Watasumi

Know that the Art of Ninzuwu is the alchemy of Fire and Water among all things. It is for this reason that during the stages of initiation, the Soul of Fire is taught first, then the Opening of the Sea. There is much wisdom in the Sea and the exploration of its depths yields the power of the hexagram and the emotions. It is known that the Opening of the Sea, once learned, is the first rite of the Temple. It is written in the Ivory Tablets of the Crow:

"The Opening of the Sea must precede all operations given with the formulae listed herein. It is the Art of Fire and Water, which began in the cities of Vasuh and Ut.."

The Lord of the Sea is known, in the ever-existing world, as Quf. It is written in the Ivory Tablets of the Crow:

"Quf agreed with what the fiery ones had spoken concerning the creation of a world that exits in time. He went down to the River of Shadows and dipped his finger in the Egu. With one drop of water he created a dimension that rested between the worlds of death and immortality."

There is much wisdom that can be found beneath the Sea, and it is the hidden place of the Beast of Muh, which can give one the anointing power over the Waters. It is written in the Ivory Tablets of the Crow:

"*The fiery ones created a beast named Muh, who is known as the Bull of Heaven in the legends of men, and they filled his veins with the green elixir. The beast came to life and was able to send foretelling dreams and special powers to the offspring of the fiery ones. The beast was placed in a region that is not visible to the eyes of men for fear that some of these would try to gain power over it. It is said that the name of this place is called Vasuh and Ut, the twin cities of water and fire, recorded in the histories of men, as the Tree of Life. The children of the fiery ones are called Hahun, They hear the voice of their forefathers resonating throughout the societies of men.* ↳↗ *! But during the beginning of the last age, certain priests, who were mortal, felt resentment against the children of the fiery ones. They learned the blasphemy of damnation and would recite the incantations and spells in reverse, which closed the doors to the outer worlds, while deceiving the children of men by their showy display and righteous character. Their deception and trickery is not easy to say in words, but it can be known because of their belief in one god.*

Before the Throne of Quf lies an eternal flame called the Oracle of Fire. The Oracle says that when Muh rises men will be filled with anger and ready to rage war against the gods, but man will not prevail, neither will the priests of men who have betrayed our sacred ways, the sons of Aho."

Know that the Lord of the Waters was known in ancient times as Watasumi. The Legend of the Tide Jewels is the history of the Opening of the Sea ceremony.

The Yi Jing Apocrypha of Genghis Khan

Origin of the Opening of the Sea Ceremony

Now in the days before Emperor Jimmu, there existed among his ancestral records the Legend of the Tide Jewels, which is the story of the Opening of the Sea ceremony. There arose two brothers, the elder brother, named Honosusori-no-Mikoto, had by nature the skill of fishing and the younger brother, named Hikohohodemi-no-Mikoto, had by nature the gift of hunting. In the beginning the two brothers, the elder and the younger, began to bargain with each other, saying: "Let us for a trial exchange gifts." They eventually exchanged them, but neither of them gained anything by doing so. The elder brother repented from the bargain he made with his younger brother, and returned to the younger brother his bow and arrows. Honosusori-no-Mikoto asked for his fish-hook to be given back to him. But the younger brother, Hikohohodemi-no-Mikoto, had already lost the elder brother's fish-hook, and had no means of finding it.

Hikohohodemi-no-Mikoto made a new fish-hook, which he offered to his elder brother. But Honosusori-no-Mikoto refused to accept it and demanded the old hook back. The younger brother was grieved by the dispute and took his cross-sword and forged from it new fish-hooks, which he heaped up in a winnowing tray, and offered these to his brother. But his elder brother, Honosusori-no-Mikoto, was angry and said: "This is not my old fish-hook! You have offered many fish-hooks, but I will not accept any of these!" Honosusori-no-Mikoto repeatedly demanded that his fish-hook be returned.

Hikohohodemi-no-Mikoto was overwhelmed with grief and be went to the shore to practice the Opening of the Sea ceremony. During this time he met one of the Ninzuwu in the person of an elderly man named Shihotsutsu-no-Oji. The old man inquired about his

177

condition, saying: "Why dost thou grieve here?"
Hikohohodemi-no-Mikoto answered the elder and told
him all that occurred between him and his eldest brother
Honosusori-no-Mikoto. The old man said: "Grieve no
more. I will straighten this matter out." Shihotsutsu-no-
Oji made a basket and placed Hohohodemi-no-Mikoto in
it.

 Hikohohodemi-no-Mikoto journeyed into the ocean
depths in the basket made for him by the Ninzuwu. He
found himself at a beautiful garden beneath the Seas,
where he abandoned the basket and proceeded on his
way, suddenly arriving at the palace of the Sea-lord
Watatsumi.

This Palace of Watatsumi was a sight to behold, as it
was nothing like anything that Hikohohodemi-no-
Mikoto had ever witnessed. Before the gate of the palace
was a well, and over the well there grew a many-
branched cassia-tree with wide-spreading boughs and
leaves. Now Hikohohodemi-no-Mikoto went up to the
foot of this tree to observe the beauty of all that was
around him. After some time a beautiful woman
appeared, and, pushing open the door, her presence came
forth. She at length took a jewel-vessel and approached
the well. She was about to draw water when she noticed
Hikohohodemi-no-Mikoto. The woman was quite
frighten by the presence of this stranger and ran back
into the palace. She spoke to her father and mother,
saying: "There is a stranger at the foot of the tree before
the gate." Watatsumi, the Lord of the Sea, thereupon
prepared an *eightfold-cushion* and let Hikohohodemi-
no-Mikoto in. When they had taken their seats,
Watasumi had inquired about his purpose in visiting
their palace. Then Hikohohodemi-no-Mikoto explained
to the Sea-lord all that transpired between him and his
eldest brother.

The Sea-lord gathered the fishes, both great and small
and required an answer from them all. The fishes
replied, saying: "We know not. Only the Red-woman has

178

had a sore mouth for some time and is not present here
with us." She was therefore summoned by the Sea-lord to
appear and upon examination of her mouth the lost hook
was found.

After this, Hikohohodemi-no-Mikoto married the Sea-
lord's daughter, Toyotamahime, and dwelt in the sea-
palace. For three years he enjoyed peace and pleasure,
but still had a longing for his own country and sighed
deeply because of such. Toyotamahime saw her husband's
grief and told her father, saying: "The Heavenly Grand-
child often sighs as if in grief. It may be that it is the
sorrow of absence from his country." Watatsumi, the
Lord of the Sea, spoke to Hikohohodemi-no-Mikoto,
addressing him in an easy and familiar way, saying: "If
the Heavenly Grand-child desires to return to his
country I will send him back." So he gave
Hikohohodemi-no-Mikoto the fish-hook which he had
found, and in doing so instructed him, saying: "When
thou givest this fish-hook to thy elder brother, before
giving it to him call to it secretly, and say, 'A poor
hook.'" Watatsumi, the Lord of the Waters, gave
Hikohohodemi-no-Mikoto the jewel of the flowing tide
and the jewel of the ebbing tide, and instructed him,
saying: "If thou dost dip the tide-flowing jewel, the tide
will suddenly flow, and thou shalt drown thine elder
brother. But in case thy elder brother should repent and
beg for forgiveness, on the contrary, thou dip the tide-
ebbing jewel, the tide will spontaneously ebb, and thou
shalt save him. If thou harass him in this way, thy elder
brother will of his own accord render submission.

When the Heavenly Grand-child was about to set out to
return to his country, Toyotamahime addressed him,
saying: "I am pregnant, and the time of my delivery is
not far off. On a day when the winds and waves are
raging, I will surely come forth to the sea-shore, and I
pray that thou wilt make for me a parturition-house, and
await me there."

When Hikohohodemi-no-Mikoto returned to his palace, he complied implicitly with the instructions of the Watatsumi, and the elder brother, Honosusori-no-Mikoto, finding himself in the utmost straits, of his own accord admitted his offense, and said: "Henceforward I will be thy subject to perform mimic dances for thee. I beseech thee mercifully to spare my life." Thereupon Hikohohodemi-no-Mikoto listened to his petition and spared his elder brother. This Honosusori-no-Mikoto was the first ancestor of the Kimi of Wobashi in Ata.

After this, Toyotamahime fulfilled her promise, also bringing with her younger sister, Tamayorihime with her, bravely they confronted the winds and waves and came to the sea-shore. When the time of her delivery was at hand, she besought Hikohohodemi-no-Mikoto, saying: "When thy handmaiden is in travail, I pray thee do not look upon her." However, the Heavenly Grand-child could not restrain himself, but went secretly and peeped in. Now Toyotamahime was just in childbirth, and had changed into a dragon. She was greatly ashamed and said: "Hadst thou not disgraced me, I would have made the sea and land communicate with each other and forever prevented them from being sundered. But now that thou hast disgraced me, wherewithal shall friendly feelings be knit together?"

When the child was born, the Heavenly Grand-child approached Toyotamahime and made inquiry saying: "By what name ought the child to be called?" She answered and said: "Let him be called Hikonagisatakeugayafukiahezu-no-Mikoto." Having said so, she took her departure straight across the sea. Then Hikohohodemi-no-Mikoto made a song, saying:

> Whatever befalls me,
> Ne'er shall I forget my love
> With whom I slept
> In the islands of wild-ducks --

The birds of the offing."

Now the formula for the Waters of Watatsumi, the Lord of the Sea, must occur in the same fashion stated earlier in this writing. The Opening of the Sea must occur. The Soul of Fire prayer and the Calling of the Shamuzi must occur. Afterwards, invoke Wutzki and recite the following formula three times:

Whoo-nn-bee eehzz-Watatsumi, moo-ah-ooh-zz-nn-eh-ph-whoo-nn-bee-moo-ah-whoo-nn-bee eehzz.

Whoo-nn-bee eehzz-Kan, moo-ah-ooh-zz-nn-eh-ph-whoo-nn-bee-moo-ah=whoo-nn-bee eehzz.

Now the formula for the Watasumi is as follows:

Watatsumi (3rd line)
Beast of Muh (2nd line)
Aum (1st line)

There are many writings by those claiming to know the Waters, but this is a lie made by those with no compassion. There is always something to learn while abiding by the Waters of Watatsumi.

Third Hexagram

The Water of Midzuhanome

Zhun

Lady: Midzuhanome

(Shki) Obstacles in the way of ambitions, (Zhee) but all is obtainable by a righteous course of action.

The Third Letter of Genghis Khan to the Magicians of the Yi Jing:

If the Mind perceives such difficulty, then it becomes a difficulty. However, all difficulties are the required steps needed to reach one's ambition.

It is not easy for a Lady to keep up her pleasant appearance and smile. It is required of her to do so in order to reach the goal set forth by Heaven and Earth. Study the way of the Lady for she is indeed a lord that rules over her affairs and can gather trustworthy assistance just by her glance alone. This can be easily seen, but the unseen hardship is not known, or the disappointment that she may hold in her heart. Yet, the Lady must awaken every morning and work on preparing herself early in the day. She is the Lady and is able to reach her ambitions because of such.

Fifth Hexagram

The Water of Susanoo

Xu

Lord: Susanoo

(Phe) Levitation of Water, or clouds appearing in Heaven, (Tuu) is an opportunity to revitalize the Soul (Nzu) by the enjoyment of life itself.

The Fifth Letter of Genghis Khan to the Magicians of the Yi Jing:

Know that the Lords of the Sea understand the importance of balance in all things. How can a man be a spiritual man if he cannot enjoy life itself?

There is also the work of nourishment. It is a work that has been recorded since the times of remote antiquity and celebrated in different forms.

We receive nourishment in the rites of the Ninzuwu. The ancestors bless us with the Food of Heaven, appearing like the Clouds of Heaven, so that we can sustain ourselves against the demons that attack the vitality of the body. This is the meaning of waiting and nourishment. And you must gather thy forces and strength together during these periods of reflection. This is the meaning of the Sword of the Ninzuwu. It is written in the Ivory Tablets of the Crow:

"*Know that the realm of the Ninzuwu is a place of mirrors above and below, side by side. It is a world of reflection, but the Ninzuwu walk about in this Dream as upon solid ground.*

There is much knowledge in this realm, for when the Sword is given to thee in the dream, one can read the thoughts of others and the moments of life become long. The planets and stars will speak to thee in dreams."

Now the Sword of the Ninzuwu was recovered by the Lord Susanoo-no-Mikoto, also known as Lord Susanoo, in ancient times. And the Sword of the Ninzuwu is also known as the Kusanagi. The knowledge of this I will impart to thee.

The Yi Jing Apocrypha of Genghis Khan

Story of the Sword of Ninzuwu

During the times of the great emperors, Susanoo-no-Mikoto went down and came to the head-waters of the River Ye, in the province of Aki. There the Lord Ashinazutenadzu resided by the River Ye along with his wife who is called Inada-no-Miyanushi-Susa-no-yatsumimi. Now the Lord Ashinazutenadzu's wife, Inada-no-Miyanushi-Susa-no-yatsumimi was pregnant with child, but the husband and wife grieved. They spoke to Lord Susanoo, saying: "Though we have had many children born to us, whenever one is born, an *eight-forked serpent* comes and devours the child, and we have not been able to save any of our children. We are about to have another child and we fear that our child will be devoured like the others. This is why we grieve."

Lord Susanoo listened intently to the husband and wife's concern. He instructed the husband and wife, saying: "Take the fruit of all kinds, and brew from it eight jars of sake, and I will kill the serpent for you.' The husband and wife followed Lord Susanoo's instructions and prepared the sake. When the time came for the child to be born, the serpent came to the door and was about to devour the child. But Lord Susanoo addressed the serpent, saying: "You are an awesome force indeed! Can I dare to neglect to feed thee?" Lord Susanoo took the eight jars of sake and poured one into each of the serpent's mouths. The serpent drank it and fell asleep. Lord Susanoo then took out his sword and slew the serpent. When he tried to sever the serpent's tail, Lord Susanoo noticed that his sword was slightly notched. He split the tail open and examined it, and found that there was a sword inside the serpent's tail. This sword is called Kusanagi But, the Ninzuwu originally named the sword, Ame-no-Murakumo-no-Tsurugi, which means "Sword of

187

the Gathering Clouds of Heaven." Lord Susanoo gave the sword to Amaterasu Omikami as a sign of repentance.

The Yi Jing Apocrypha of Genghis Khan

Eighth Hexagram

The Water of Nudzuwata

＃∨ ℓ∿

Bi

Lady: Nudzuwata

＃∨ ℓ∿

(Tuu) The woman who walks upon the waters
(Zhee) and blesses the land is she.

The Eighth Letter of Genghis Khan to the Magicians of the Yi Jing:

The Lady completes her preparations before the rising
sun. By her charm she is able to establish a place in the
heavens. Her smile is worth more than many precious
metals. However, it is by reason of her virtue that she is
cherished among the nations of men, and these do honor
her as a symbols of their law.

It is the Water upon the fertile soil that makes way for a
great harvest. Now the merchants of the land will use her
image to attract the business of Fool. Though they may
reap a harvest from among the ignorant, the true Lord

knows the alchemy of such fates and counts all that he
has received, respectfully, and with due honor of the
Lady.

Twenty-Ninth Hexagram

The Water of Watasumi

५⋗ 丬
Kan

Ruler: Watasumi

५⋗ 丬 (Aum) The calling of (Shki) dark forces is
only beneficial for beneficial purposes.

The Twenty-Ninth Letter of Genghis Khan to the Magicians of the Yi Jing:

The foundation of Ninzuwu is found in the practice of
virtue. It is for this reason that the Lady will attract
men of various honors, but she will not concede to any of
these. The Waters are deep and to walk upon them she
must maintain her virtue, or drown in whoredom, which
only lends the hand of ridicule to speak.

Know too, that the Netherworld is a place of obscure
senses, but a certain formula can be found there.
Unfortunately, the Fool will remain in the Netherworld
even though he has been told that nothing grows in this
land. The Fool will stay in this condition because he is

intoxicated by what appears to the senses and to the mind during his time of rest in the Netherworld. Yet, the blessings of life are slow and rarely come. While he may take note of these things, the Fool is still intoxicated with the Abyss. He will listen to those who do not know the way. And the Fool does not know when to escape the Netherworld, or the secret path that leads to the Heavens.

It is only by virtue that one can leave the Netherworld. Remember that the Divine-Lords are created through cleanliness, and their power is awesome in the face of the Netherworld for those of the dark region tremble in fear before the faces of those that shine.

Know that these things were known in times of remote antiquity, for it was recited as the Origin of the Fahmu. It is written in the Ivory Tablets of the Crow:

"Know that when the Sword of the Ninzuwu is received, it must be used to cut the Grasses of the Fahmu. And the Fahmu have bodies like trees with skin of flowing waters. Their land is like a desert of the skies, but it is a bright place."

I will write herein the account of the Fahmu that was recited in times of ancient antiquity:

Origins of the Fahmu

Izanagi-no-Mikoto made water against a large tree, which turned into a great river. While the Ugly Females of Yomi were preparing to cross this river, Izanagi-no-Mikoto had already reached the Even Pass of Yomi. He took a rock, large enough for a thousand men to lift and blocked up the path with it. He then stood face to face with Izanami-no-Mikoto and pronounced the formula for divorce. Upon hearing this, Izanami-no-Mikoto said: "My dear Lord and husband, if thou sayest so, I will strangle to death the people of the country which doest govern, a thousand in one day." Then Izanagi-no-Mikoto replied, saying: "My beloved younger sister, if thou sayest so, I will in one day cause fifteen-hundred to be born." Izanagi-no-Mikoto continued: "Come no further!"

Izanagi-no-Mikoto threw down his staff that was called Funado-no-Kami. He threw down his girdle that was called Nagachiha-no-Kami. Moreover, he threw down his upper garment, which was called Wadzurahi-no-Kami. He threw down his trousers, which were called Akigui-no-Kami. He threw down his shoes, which were called Chishiki-no-Kami.

Some say that the Even Pass of Yomi is not any place in particular, but means only the space of time when the breath fails on the approach of death.

Now the rock that blocked the Even Pass of Yomi was called Yomido-ni-fusagaru-Ohkami, also called Chigayeshi-no-Ohkami.

When Izanagi-no-Mikoto had returned, he felt regret, saying: "Having gone to Yomi, the Netherworld, a hideous and filthy place, it is necessary that I should

cleanse my body from its pollutions." He accordingly
went to the plain of Ahagi at Tachibana in Wodo in
Hiuga of Tsukushi, and purified himself. Just as he was
about to wash away the impurities of his body, he yelled:
"The upper stream is too rapid and the lower stream is
too sluggish, I will wash in the middle stream." The God
which was thereby produced is called Yasomagatsubi-no-
Kami, meaning "eighty-evils of the body," and then to
remedy these evils there were produced the Lords
Kaminawobi-no-Kami, and after him Ohonawobi-no-
Kami.

Now the Lords that were produced from Izanagi-no-
Mikoto's purification, washing at the bottom of the sea,
were called Sokotsuwatatsumi-no-Mikoto and Sokatsutu-
no-Mikoto. Moreover, when washed in mid-tide, there
were Lords produced called Nakatsuwatadzumi-no-
Mikoto and Nakatsusuwo-no-Mikoto. When Izanagi-no-
Mikoto purified himself on the surface of the Water, the
Lords Uhatsuwatadzumi-no-Mikoto and Uhatsutsuwo-
no-Mikoto were produced. *There were in all nine Gods.*

And it was by the act of purification that Izanagi-no-
Mikoto was able to produce many marvelous things.
Know that the Fahmu are the roads of energy that run
through thy body, and these too must be purified and cut
with the Sword of the Ninzuwu. It is like Water staring
at itself in the mirror. What appears to be deep may not
be deep at all, just a corruption of the mind. No matter
what they do, or what they say, the Fool will always seek
the justification and pleasure of ignorance in order to
validate his own existence.

Thirty-Ninth Hexagram

The Water of Ugajin

Jian

Lord: Ugajin

(Phe) In the face of an obstacle, (Bnhu) it is time to look within oneself (Shki) and correct errors.

The Thirty-Ninth Letter of Genghis Khan to the Magicians of the Yi Jing:

Good fortune is a work of refinement. Some people are lucky and never learn anything in life. Good fortune is a work of refinement. This is a most necessary work in thy undertakings.

This work is very similar to the law of the traveling merchants. Be careful not to give more than what your word can hold. You hear these words, but still you do not understand.

When the mind gives way to thoughts about pleasing one's desires more than using the energy of the mind to refine one's character, obstacles will arise. This is the Law of Obstacles. Obstacles increase when we think more about our wants than our needs. This is the lesson of the Quekanuit.

Now the history of the Quekanuit is known among the Magicians of the Yi Jing since the times of remote antiquity. It is written in the Ivory Tablets of the Crow:

"Quekanuit is the said to be the Empty Space of the Warrior. It is a place that is empty of images and things usually perceived by the mind. When the spirit enters Quekanuit, the mind of thee will take a thousand forms. It is because of this reason that many call it the Dream of the Same Faces. Know that when you enter this realm, thou will see an army of souls, and each soul is a deed that though has performed in life. Some of these souls will be sad and others are happy. Some deeds will lust after their own selves. Every deed that one has performed will be seen by one, whether it be good or bad."

Know that in ancient times the Quekanuit was known in the societies of men as Quikinna'qu, father of Cana'inuit. Understand the Lesson of Quikinna'qu.

The Yi Jing Apocrypha of Genghis Khan

The Origin of the Quekanuit

Quikinna'qu, also known as the Big Raven, and his son Eme'mqut took note that it had been raining for many days, so they decided to visit Tenanto'mwan on the plains of existence to find out what was the cause of the ongoing rain. They put on their raven feathers and took flight over the Land of Existence. While flying above Tenanto'mwan's home, they heard the sound of a drum.

Quikinna'qu, also known as the Big Raven, the father-shaman, and his son Eme'mqut, entered the house of Tenanto'mwan and found the husband with his wife, the Rain Woman. The husband cutoff his wife's vulva and attached it to the drum. Tenanto'mwan also cut off his own penis and was using it like a drumstick to beat the vulva, from which water poured onto the earth below, creating the continuous rainfall. When Tenanto'mwan saw Quikinna'qu, the Big Raven, and his son Eme'mqut, he stopped beating the drum and put his instruments away. The rain ceased. Quikinna'qu and Eme'mqut pretended to leave the house, but instead overcame their shape and took the disguise of mats made of reindeer hair and laid down on the floor. When Tenanto'mwan saw that he and his wife were alone, he took out his drum again and began making it rain once more.

While still in the other form, Quikinna'qu spoke to Eme'mqut about casting a spell to make Tenanto'mwan fall asleep. He instructed Eme'mqut, that he must watch where Tenanto'mwan places the drum and drumstick before going to sleep. Soon after, Tenanto'mwan puts the instruments aside. Tenanto'mwan and the Rain Woman fell asleep under the magical spell of Quikinna'qu. Quikinna'qu took the drum and drumstick while the husband and wife were sleeping and roasted them over a fire until they were dry. Quikinna'qu then replaced the instruments.

197

After Tenanto'mwan awakened, he started to beat the
drum again, not knowing that the instruments were
replaced by Quikinna'qu. In so doing, the weather turned
bright and the Sun appeared. The longer Tenanto'mwan
beat the drum, the longer the weather remained dry.
Quikinna'qu and Eme'mqut returned home, but as the
days continued, the hunting got poor and the people
began to starve.

Quikinna'qu returned to the house of Tenanto'mwan to
discuss the problems that have occurred in the land.
Tenanto'mwan felt regret about his lack of compassion
and promised Quikinna'qu that the hunting will become
pleasant again. When Quikinna'qu returned home, he
saw that the harvest was good. He remembered the words
of Tenanto'mwan and saw that it went accordingly.
Quikinna'qu then made the necessary sacrifices in front
of the Lords of the Crows and the tribe prospered once
again.

Forty-Eighth Hexagram

The Water of Ama-no-Uzume

Jing

Lady: Ama-no-Uzume

(Hmu) People may come and go, but sexual energy, like the Well of the village, (Shki) runs deep. (Aum) Once called, this energy rises up as it may. Hmu (4) plus Shki (9) plus Aum (2) is the number of the goddess, fifteen.

The Forty-Eighth Letter of Genghis Khan to the Magicians of the Yi Jing:

The Lady knows that the history of man is the history of an unseen law. Things appear to change, but the transformation of moods and emotions in one's environment is based on the unseen ruler of all experience, the sexual energy.

The measurement of this energy is known and the Book of Changes is an operation which can calculate the position of the sexual force at any given time. The Well is the menstrual cycle of the Lady, for it is the number forty-eight. Know that the changes of Heaven and Earth are the polarities of the full and new moons, and that the sign of the full moon is always opposite the sign of the new moon in the space of one month. It has been this way since the days of remote antiquity.

Now the full moon is the line of yang and the new moon is the line of yin. Know that in the space of one month, two lines are produced. But, in the space of forty-eight days three lines are produced. These things appeared before the creation of man and were known as the Menstruating-Woman among the race of men soon after.

In the world before, which presently exists, these things were taught as the Law of the Ayaqox. It is written in the Ivory Tablets of the Crow:

"Ayaqox the Great Woman was known as a Seductress in the world before man. She often changes shape to appear attractive to the mind of an Initiate. Sometimes Ayaqox will appear as a handsome man to a woman full of desire. Other times, she will appear to the man of great vigor, as a beautiful woman with long black hair and the face of a praying mantis with green skin… The Ayaqox is able to discern the desires of others, their motives, even though they may be hidden. But, she is also the teacher of the price of lust and knows the karma that must be paid… The reciting of Lustful Words must occur for Seven Days upon which no desirous contact can be made. After the Seven Days have passed, Ayaqox will visit thee in a dream and give unto you The Stone Bowl of Eternity."

Know that the Law of the Ayaqox was taught within the civilizations of men during times of remote antiquity. Now the Ayaqox, whose name *Aya* means *dawn*, was also known as Aoxaif, and Ana-no-Uzume, which means *dawn*.

Study well, the Law of the Ayaqox, so that thy heart may receive a favorable outcome when visiting the Well.

The Law of the Ayaqox

Now it was during the days of the struggle between Amaterasu-Omikami and her younger brother Susanoo-no-Mikoto, that Lord Susanoo did in fact vandalize the rice fields of his older sister, the Shining Lady in Heaven. Amaterasu-Omikami became furious with Lord Susanoo and took refuge in the Heavenly Rock Cave, also known as Amano-Iwato.

The Shining Lady of Heaven was seen no more and the world turned dark and cold, as none of the Lords could call forth the Shining Lady of Heaven from the Rock-cave.

Ama-no-Uzume, ancestress of Sarume-no-Kimi, skilled in the measurements of the sexual energies, picked up a spear wreathed with Eulalia grass, and standing before the door of the Rock-cave of Heaven, skillfully performed a mimic dance. Ama-no-Uzume took the true Sakaki tree of the Heavenly Mount Kagu, and made a head-dress. She took club-moss and made braces. She kindled fires and placed the tub bottom upwards, and gave forth a divinely-inspired utterance.

Now Amaterasu-OhmiKami heard the noise of Ama-no-Uzume and said to herself: "I have shut myself up in the Rock-cave, there ought surely to be continual night in the Central Land of fertile reed-plains. How can Ama-no-Uzume be so happy?" So with her august hand, she opened the Rock-cave door slightly and looked out to see what was occurring. When the Shining Lady of Heaven opened the Rock-cave door, she saw her glorious reflection in a mirror, which Ama-no-Uzume had placed on a tree, and the Shining Lady of Heaven slowly emerged from her hiding spot. Then Tajikarawo-no-

Kami took Amaterasu-Ohmikami by the hand, and led her out the cave. Soon after, Amaterasu-Ohmikami was convinced to rejoin the divine world. This is the Law of the Ayaqox.

Sixtieth Hexagram

The Water of Izanami-no-Mikoto

Jie

Lady: Izanami-no-Mikoto

(Nzu) Water over Lake. (Phe) Success can be achieved from restraint and the course of discipline, (Shki) but it is to no benefit to remain in a harsh environment.

The Sixtieth Letter of Genghis Khan to the magicians of the Yi Jing:

The Lady will establish methods of the unknown in conjunction with the ways of Heaven and Earth and exercise a spirit of restraint that is not excessive in nature.

The simplicity of the Lady is a mystery among the civilizations of man and there are less words to be said over many things.

The Yi Jing Apocrypha of Genghis Khan

The Lady exercises the Art of Articulation as a form of sacrifice to the Lord of Restraint that harsh conditions may not come upon thee by chance. The Art of Articulation is how the Lady ensures enough food for her family. Calculation and measuring the wheat were regulations taught to the Initiates as the Measurement of Zasosu. It is written in the Ivory Tablets of the Crow:

"The Zasosu can give one a desire or take it away. They are the Lords of Impatience and Hesitation, and rule men through such. Some men have stayed in the Realms of the Zasosu and never perform any new task. But the Zasosu can also increase the Will of a man and the strength they hold within their hearts."

The Yi Jing Apocrypha of Genghis Khan

The History of Zasosu

Know that in the societies of men, Zasosu was known as
the wife of Zao Jun. It has been said that these things
occurred in the world before, but take place in the time
of man so that the measurements of such may be learned.

Now there existed a woman who knew the force of the
Dragon Lords and had maintained congress with them
for many years.

Eventually, the woman, who is called Zasosu, a daughter
of the spirit-people who dwell beyond the veils, felt
sorrow in her heart. She observed the ways of the women
living in her village for over one-hundred years, but
knew not the ways of motherhood. She would often cry to
herself, saying: "Is there no man for me? Is there no man
for me that I may conceive a child?"

Now it was that Zasosu, and those of her race, did not
give way to age. Soon the people in the village took note
that her beauty never faded and accused her of being a
witch. Accordingly, Zasosu would only leave her house
during the night and never made her presence known to
the people of the village thereafter. The people of the
village spoke among themselves, saying: "The witch is no
longer! She must surely have died from hunger!" Over
time the people who knew of Zasosu passed away and
those that followed them thought of such things as
fables.

Now it came about that a merchant, with a great
knowledge of spices was traveling through the village
and needed to rest. Nearing the village, he saw a house
that appeared to be abandoned and knocked on the door.
After knocking for some time, he opened the door and
took to rest near the entrance of the house, as it was still

daylight. Now Zasosu would awaken in the evening so as to avoid any the people of the village.

Now the man had slept loudly and this had awakened Zasosu. She hurried through the house and searched out the source of the loudness and discovered the merchant sleeping near the entrance of the house.

Zasosu was quite startled to see the merchant and retrieved her sword. She called the merchant from his sleep and questioned him fiercely, saying: "Why have you entered the house of Zasosu?" The merchant grew afraid, but admired the beauty of Zasosu and her radiance. The merchant was hesitant to respond, but knew the fate of silence. He stood up and spoke with a calmly face, saying: "I have only spices to sell on this journey and sought a place to rest after many days. I am Ju from the village across the water."

The merchant Ju did persuade Zasosu with a calmly voice. Shortly after, they became husband and wife. Zasosu conceived a child and her husband, the merchant Ju, began to travel on the road again as a means of caring for his family.

While traveling by ship, the heart of the merchant Ju began to betray his wife Zasosu. After some months had passed, the merchant Ju made preparations to take another wife and leave Zasosu.

When the merchant Ju told Zasosu his plans for divorce, Zasosu did change in appearance. Her face became like that of a dragon and Zasosu cursed Ju, saying: "You will see my face before you die!" The merchant Ju gathered his things swiftly and never returned to the house of Zasosu again.

So it was that the merchant Ju did take up marriage with a younger woman. And the younger woman demanded many things, and the merchant Ju came under much distress. After returning from a long journey Ju decided to take a rest in the garden underneath the light of the Sun. Suddenly, Ju became stricken with fear as everything around him had grown dark. The merchant called out to his wife, the young woman, thinking that he slept for long hours and had awakened in the night. His wife, however, was stricken with grief and shame. She chastised Ju, saying: "It is not night! It is day and not night! Surely, you must be blind! How can a blind man please me?" And the wife of the merchant Ju demand a divorce from him and did claim the land that he acquired for herself. The merchant Ju was forced to take up the ways of a beggar.

The merchant Ju was no longer sought after for spices that he once bargained and sold. People felt saddened by the fate that Ju had acquired. And the people of the village would feed him, and some of the people would make mockery of Ju because they didn't know him as a merchant.

Ju had taken to a different place in the village. One woman, upon seeing that Ju was hungry, invited him to her house for a meal. Ju was pleased with the meal he had eaten, saying: "I have not eaten food like this for many years. The wife of my youth, the woman Zasosu, made such a meal as this." The woman listened intently to the words of Ju.

Ju began to feel the pain of regret for all the sin he had committed against Zasosu. He began weeping fiercely over these things and was saddened by the course he took during his youth. Now the woman upon hearing the words of Ju felt sad and could see his change of heart. She spoke to Ju, saying: "You can open your eyes now!" Ju opened his eyes and he saw that the woman, who had taken him for a meal, was the wife Zasosu.

Ju felt so much shame upon seeing his former wife Zasosu that he threw himself into the kitchen fire and became like the incense of merchants. Zasosu tried to save him, but his spirit was called forth in service to the other worlds, and as the guardian spirit of Zasosu, and their children. He became known to the nations as the husband of Zasosu and from that day forward as Zao Jun.

Sixty-Third Hexagram

The Water of Ajisukitakahikone

Ji Ji

Lord: Ajisukitakahikone

(Aum) The ability to create a good experience (Nzu) is the best weapon against misfortune. Water over Fire.

The Sixty-Third Letter of Genghis Khan to the Magicians of the Yi Jing:

The acquisition of immortality is a very simple equation. Is it possible for the practitioner of these sacred arts to become something more than the sum of their experience? This is the equation of immortality. Experience is the fate of the stars and in thy study of the

principal aspects of one's initiation it can be determined
what experiences are created by the initiate, and those
that are cast upon thee by the stars. It is not a rebellious
action, but is written as such in the libraries of men. The
Magician is married to the Universe. It is his bride. It is
the Lady and for the Priestess it is her husbandly owner.

In the beginning of this relationship the Universe will
call upon its Lover and reveal to its Lover methods that
the Magician and the Priestess can use to evolve. But the
Universe has many Lovers in this regard, and due to
such, was recorded in the history of Fools as a spiritual
whore. What the Fool doesn't know is that the Universe
seeks to raise a Lover up for itself that is equal to the
Universe in stature and strength. In this way, the
Universe can breathe the Spirit of Water into its Lover
and the Lover can absorb the force and reciprocate the
same as Fire. This is the meaning of life even among the
uninitiated who are left unaware of its purpose.

They themselves, however, understand their place in the
scheme of things and know that they are dependent upon
the life of the Universe. This is the lesson of the Iwuvh.
It is written in the Ivory Tablets of the Crow:

*"The Iwuvh are born from the storms that occur in the
land. When they perish, the Iwuvh return to the body of
the storm and are born again. The length of their life is as
long as a flash of lightening, but the Initiate must obtain
the Body of Iwuvh and have intercourse with it, for the
Eye that it sits upon is the Eye of Knowing."*

Acquiring the Eye of Knowing is a process and when it
is obtained, one can use such to create their own
experience. This is not achieved by some ritual, but must
come in the way of things that are natural, like the milk
from a woman's breast nourishing her child. Thy course
of virtue is also one of nourishment. Yet the initiation

must take place in stillness. This is the History of the Iwuvh.

The Yi Jing Apocrypha of Genghis Khan

The History of the Iwuvh

Now the Body of the Iwuvh is a symbol of the Universe
and so it is spoken about in a peculiar manner in the
Ivory Tablets of the Crow. Know too, that in the
civilizations of man the Iwuvh is known as Iaru and was
said to be ruled by a great king after he resurrected
himself from the Netherworld. But the formula of
Iwuvh, which is the formula for its use, was revealed
during the days of remote antiquity.

Amaterasu-Omikami gave the command unto
Amewakahiko, saying: "The Central land of Reed-Plains
is a region for my child to rule over. Considering,
however, that there are certain rebellious, violent, and
wicked Deities, do thou therefore go first and subdue it."
Accordingly she gave him the Heavenly deer-bow and
the Heavenly true deer-arrows and sent him off.

Amewakahiko after receiving the command from
Amaterasu-Omikami, went down and did marry many
daughters of the Earthly Lords. *Eight years* passed,
Amewakahiko failed to give any report concerning his
mission. Amaterasu-Omikami, concerned about the
matter, summoned Omohikane-no-Kami, also known as
the *Thought-Combining* deity, and inquired as to why
Amewakahiko did not return or give report. Now the
Thought-Combining deity spent time in meditation and
spoke to Amaterasu-Omikami, saying; "It will be good to
send a pheasant to investigate this matter further."
Accordingly, Amaterasu-Omikami took the Thought-
Combining deity's advice and a pheasant was sent to
investigate the matter.

The pheasant flew down and landed on top of a many-
branched cassia-tree, which stood before Amewakahiko's

gate. The pheasant uttered a loud cry, saying:
"Amewakahiko! Where have you been for the past *eight
years* that you should give no report to the Lady of
Heaven?" Now a certain Divine Lady of Earth named
Amanosagume, saw the pheasant, and turned to
Amewakahiko, saying: "A bird of evil cry is sitting on
top of this tree. It will be well to shoot it and kill it. So
Amewakahiko took the Heavenly deer-bow and the
Heavenly true deer-arrow given to him by the Heavenly
Lady and shot it, upon which the arrow went through
the pheasant's breast and reached the place where the
Heavenly Lady was.

Upon seeing the arrow, Amaterasu-Omikami spoke to
herself, saying: "This is the arrow that I gave to
Amewakahiko. Why is it here?" Amaterasu-Omikami
took the arrow, and pronounced a curse over it: "If this
arrow has been shot with an evil intent, let mischief
come upon Amewakahiko; but if it has been shot with a
tranquil heart, let no harm befall him." She flung the
arrow down and it struck Amewakahiko in the chest and
he died immediately after. This is the reason why people
at the present day say, 'Fear a returning arrow.'

Now Amewakahiko's wife and children came down from
Heaven and went away upwards, taking the dead body
with them. Then they made a mourning house in
Heaven, which they placed the body that they lamented
in. Upon hearing the news, Ajisukitakahikone-no-Kami,
a good friend of Amewakahiko, ascended to Heaven and
mourned with the family. Now Ajisukitakahikone-no-
Kami had the exact appearance as Amewakahiko.
Therefore, Amewakahiko's wife and children, when they
saw Ajisukitakahione-no-Kami, thought Amewakahiko
was still alive and began to rejoice, saying: "Our Lord is
still alive." And they clung to his robe and to his girdle,
and could not be thrust away. Ajisukitakahikone-no-
Kami became angry and said: "My friend is dead and I

have come to make condolence. Why should I be mistaken for a dead man?"
Ajisukitakahikone-no-Kami drew out his ten-span sword and cut down the house of mourning, which fell to Earth and became a mountain.

The Heavens of Johuta

Understand that true immortality is an art. One must respect what is alive as an extension of unseen things. The Fool seeks to remain forever in a temporary place, which is completely unnatural.

There is peace in the Heavens of Johuta. Only Fools will debate the understanding of the position for what is yang is the light of the Divine-Lady and what is yin is the shadow of the Divine Lady. Is it not so that a woman carries the male child for nine months? Is it not true that the Universe carries a male child in her womb also? If the Earth is not Heaven then there is no way for us to evolve. If a man is born of Earth; is it not his purpose to become a Man of Heaven?

It is very simple. In Heaven, a woman is an aspiring bride. On Earth, a woman is preparing to distribute nourishment for the rest of her family. It is written in the Ivory Tablets of the Crow:

"After the birth of Johuta, the people in the village began to make gossip, concerning Nudzuchi, and accused her of practicing necromancy, since Johuta, like Xuz, was black."

Know that the meaning of Johuta is in many things which pertain to the three aspects of the innermost mind, and this mind must also include the other two. And the Heavens are still part of the eight and its door must be opened with the following formula:

216

Moo-ah-moo-ah-eek-hss-you-mmh-ha-eh-ph Johuta,
whoo-nn-bee eehzz!

 Johuta !

Moo-ah-moo-ah-eek-hss-you-mmh-ha-eh-ph Qian,
whoo-nn-bee eehzz!

These words must be recited twelve times after the
Opening of the Sea has been performed and the Soul of
Fire must be called, then the rite of the Shamuzi. Also
summon Ninzuwu and Wutzki. This is the map of
Johuta:

Johuta (3rd line)
Baptism of the Ancient One (2nd line)
Zhee (1st line)

The Heavens are pure and one cannot exist in this realm,
or visit such, without virtue. The beauty of Heaven is in
its simplicity. The aspects of Heaven are without
division, as it includes the names of many things that
stretch beyond the border of one nation. The Divine Ones
do not divide themselves up in the same way that men do.
Things of this nature are evil. The Fool is still left
unaware that when the nature of a man is drawn to evil
things, he is under the control of an evil force. It is for
this reason that Heaven was made and carefully

constructed by those pure of heart, so that the Garden of Immortality can be understood.

First Hexagram

The Heaven of Kotoamatsukami

Qian

Kotoamatsukami

(Zhee) Birth of an idea is in motion. (Shki) Strength in action is the sum of the outcome.

The First Letter of Genghis Khan to the Magicians of the Yi Jing:

Heaven is the throne of responsibility. Pursue such things with honor. The path is very simple. What exists in Heaven is not burdensome, and when one gives way to such thoughts, they have fallen from grace. How much time does a bird spend making its nest? Does it seek to rest during such times of adversity? Surely, a wager made during hardship is the training needed to remain in Heaven.

Sixth Hexagram

The Heaven of Suzha

Song

Crow: Suzha

(Hmu) When stress is in motion (Shki) meditate on the beginning of the experience.

The Sixth Letter of Genghis Khan to the Magicians of the Yi Jing:

During the days of old, stress was likened to rain falling from Heaven. It can cause a delay in the daily chores of life. But the Waters of Heaven are needed to make things grow. After the rain has fallen, the light of the goddess nurtures the crops. Life is the same.

When the mind has become a temple of worries, know that it is raining. It is during this time that you must push the clouds away from the heart and hold an image in your mind of the blessing. Use each and every opportunity of conflict as a time to hurl an arrow into the hunt.

Tenth Hexagram

The Heaven of Kamuy-Zi

Lu

Crow: Kamuy-Zi

(Lewhu) Begin at the beginning. Exercise caution in consideration of the affairs of other people.

The Tenth Letter of Genghis Khan to the Magicians of the Yi Jing:

The three worlds will become as one and what is unseen to many, will be readily seen in the mind's eye. Caution is the perspective of the traveler reaching an unknown plain of existence.

The Magicians of the Unseen Lands know who you are. They can reach you by entering the minds of those around you. Pay attention to these things, even the Fool knows that the sign of one's birth is evidence of star's ability to possess matter. How much more can this be accomplished by understanding the secret meaning of prayer? Hurl an arrow into the hunt. Heaven and Earth is a secret society that is often an object of imitation, but what engineer can surpass the technology that brings all things into existence? It is as simple as looking at the lines in your hand. How can you put your hands together in prayer and not know the meaning of these things?

Twelfth Hexagram

The Heaven of Kayra-jin

Pi

Crow: Kayra-Jin

 (Aum) The call of the (Shki) void over (Zhee) virtue is a harsh initiation.

The Twelfth Letter of Genghis Khan to the Magicians of the Yi Jing:

The harvest is not ripe in the season of winter. This sacred art is given to thee for the work of preservation and benefit of thy people.

Riches from unclean sources will lead to poverty and rob the spirit of its majestic heritage. There is the way, however, of the dark initiation and these evils cannot even profane such a path for the man of honor.

The Yi Jing Apocrypha of Genghis Khan

Once the yin has been offered the proper sacrifice, it must be studied with an intoxicating passion until the climax is received and all of its ways have been unveiled.

After this knowledge has been obtained, it is no longer fruitful to pursue such a course. The study of such things are only beneficial as they may creep in thy experience of despair and can easily be seen and conquered. Otherwise, they become toxins become in the body that nurtures the spirit.

Thirteenth Hexagram

The Heaven of Ichikishimahime-no-mikoto

Tong Ren

Crow: Ichikishimahime-no-mikoto

(Shki) Gathering (Aum-Zhee-Bnhu) of forces, unifying causes.

The Thirteenth Letter of Genghis Khan to the Magicians of the Yi Jing:

Heaven is just the beginning, but it is entered and understood by the union of forces. The dualistic-man cannot enter Heaven, if they cannot see the primary force moving, shaping, and forming the world, in the world, and in all phases of time.

It is a very simple equation, the shadow, the body, and the light. Are they really divided? The Birds of Heaven have gained the ability of flight by the use of two wings for a single cause.

Twenty-Fifth Hexagram

The Heaven of Ishitijin

Wu Wang

Crow: Ishitijin

(Zhee) Success is always in the company of those (Bnhu) with pure hearts.

The Twenty-Fifth Letter of Genghis Khan to the Magicians of the Yi Jing:

When the balcony of Heaven opens itself up, one can look down and see that their actions are the writings and prayers heard by the Divine-Lords. This is the lesson given to us in the Ivory Tablets of the Crow:

"And the Shamuzi will protect thee from harm and the unknowing voices that will try to enter the mind. And do not be alarmed by her appearance when she comes to greet thee and stand by thy side. Now the lower part of the Shamuzi is like a

horse and the upper part is that of a beautiful woman with long golden hair. Its eyes are like those of a cat and in its teeth are the fangs of a bat. However, its spirit is pure as a small child, for innocence is a valuable treasure that has long since been forgotten."

Know that the pure heart is the Calling of the Shamuzi, for the Shamuzi is known as the great purifier. Few men have come to the understanding that one's thoughts and emotions are prayers of the heart and the highest form of communication with those who live in the unseen lands.

Thirty-Third Hexagram

The Heaven of Naziqjin

Dun

Crow: Naziqjin

(Shki) The evil one cannot be tamed by anger.
(Phe) Yield in silence.

The Thirty-Third Letter of Genghis Khan to the Magicians of the Yi Jing:

The sacred arts were handed down to the Magicians of the Yi Jing from ancient times. The Divine-Lords only instructed those who were pure in heart. This too, is an initiation.

It is not certain if our prayer to reduce the karma of the world will answer the problems of man. But, it is certain that by the continued practice of such, the muscle of purity is strengthened and the element of divinity blossoms a little each day.

Forty-Fourth Hexagram

The Heaven of Inari-Ohkami

Gou

Crow: Inari-Ohkami

(Hmu) The ways of temptation (Hmu) is not the way of Heaven and Earth.

The Forty-Fourth Letter of Genghis Khan to the Magicians of the Yi Jing:

This work of perfection is the very thing of pleasure indeed, but do not forsake the quest for such pleasure. There is no greater form of magic than that of a clean heart and a pure mind.

When the body has fallen away from the spirit the weight of your soul, and your emotional state of being, determines the world you will live in after the world of the senses has been destroyed.

Scroll of Ishanashte

These are the Histories of the Shamuzi, and the study of these things preserves the purity and understanding of how to proceed in the course of thy work. Remember these lessons when evil beckons the mind, for in the recall of these things, unnatural forces will vacate their attempts.

Hunter of the Netherworld

During the Age of the Gods, there lived a brave young man who was a skillful hunter. The people in the world of this time, believed that the young man was an heir of the Divine-Lords. These are the scriptures of the ancient tribe of man that has survive since the days of remote antiquity. One day, the skillful hunter took to the chase of a large bear, deep in the mountains of that particular world. The bear ran endlessly, but the young hunter did not waver in his pursuit.

The young hunter remained steady in the chase and the bear was cunning in its movements, not allowing the hunter to get close enough to shoot it with poisoned arrows. At last, the bear disappeared and fell down a hole in the ground. The young hunter followed the bear and found himself in a large cave. Towards the far end of the cave was a gleam of light, and the young hunter did follow in this direction, as he found himself in another world. There existed everything that can be found in the world of man, but this was a place of unearthly beauty. There were trees, houses, villages, and human beings. The young hunter wasn't concerned about any of these things. He was still in pursuit of the bear, which had by now vanished. He thought it best to seek such in the mountains that stood in the distance of this

new underground world. The young hunter took flight
up a valley. Exhausted and hungry after the long
pursuit, the younger hunter was delighted to find the
fruit of a mulberry tree and a few grapevines nearby.

Suddenly, the young hunter was able to look at the other
side of himself and was horrified to find that he was
transformed into a snake. His cries and groans were like
the hissing noise of the snakes. In disbelief his mind was
petrified. How could he go back to the land of his
parents, where snakes were hated? He would surely die
in the attempt of such a thing. No cure for this curse
came to his mind. The young hunter had to creep back to
the entrance of the cave that led back to the world of
man. At the foot of the entrance, he saw a pine-tree of
enormous size and height, and there he fell asleep.

During his sleep, the Divine-Lady of the pine-tree
appeared to him in a dream, saying: "It saddens my heart
to see you in such a state. Why did you eat the poisonous
fruits of the Netherworld? If you climb up to the top of
this pine-tree and fling yourself down, then you may,
perhaps, become a human being again."

The younger hunter, now a snake, awakened and was
filled half with hope and half with fear. Yet, he was
determined to follow the advice of the Divine-Lady who
appeared to him in his dreams. Gliding up the tall pine-
tree, he reached the top-most branch. After hesitating for
a few moments, he flung himself down. When he
awakened from the crash, he found himself standing at
the foot of the tree. Nearby, was the body of an immense
serpent, ripped open, so as to allow the young hunter a
way to climb out of it.

The young hunter offered up thanks to the pine-tree, and
made divine symbols in its honor. He retraced his steps,
finding the way in which he entered the Netherworld.
After walking for some time, he reached the world of

men and the top of the mountain where he had first pursued the bear that he never saw again.

During the night, while the young hunter was asleep, the Divine Lady of the pine-tree appeared in his dream once more, saying:

"It is time for you to return to the Netherworld. The bear you were chasing, was a spirit-woman of the Netherworld. She deceived you in order to gain your hand in marriage. You must now return to her."

The young hunter awoke, but a terrible sickness had over powered him. A few days later he returned to the Netherworld a second time. He never returned to the land of the living.

Child of a Divine-Lord

There once lived a very beautiful woman, who was without husband. She was arranged in marriage with a traveling merchant, but they did not lie down together in bed. Nevertheless, the woman conceived a child. The woman was greatly surprised for she did not lie in the bed of pleasure with any man. The people of the village discussed this matter among themselves, saying: "She has conceived a child through lying with some other man." This is what the people of the village said. The man who was to be her husband was very angry. But he was not certain as to how she conceived a child.

The woman finally gave birth. She gave birth to a little snake. She was greatly ashamed. Her mother took the little snake, went out, and with tears in her eyes, she spoke: "What god is responsible for this act? If he should beget a child upon my daughter, it would have at least been better if it was a human child. But this little snake we human beings cannot keep. As it is the child of the god who beget it, may he well keep it." The old woman threw the snake away and went in the house of her daughter.

Afterwards there was a loud noise of a baby crying. The old woman went out, and looked. It was a beautiful baby. The old woman carried it in. The woman who had given birth to the child was delighted with tears. The baby was found to be a boy and the mother kept her son. Years passed, and the child became a man of fine appearance and very large in stature. He was a skilled hunter.

The woman who had given birth was astonished over what occurred. It was discovered that she had fell asleep in the light of the Sun, which had shone upon her

234

through the opening in the roof. Then she dreamt a
dream, which said: "I being a god, have given you a child
because I love you. When you die, you shall truly become
my wife. Our son, when he gets married, will have plenty
of children." After the dream the woman did worship.
Accordingly, her son became a great hunter and a rich
man. Eventually, the woman died without having a
human husband. Her son was blessed with a beautiful
wife and children. His descendants are still alive today.

The Yi Jing Apocrypha of Genghis Khan

The Wicked Sorcerer

One day a wizard told a man he knew that, if any one were to climb a certain mountain-peak and jump off on to the belt of clouds below, he would be able to ride on the clouds like a horse, and see the whole world. Trusting in what the wizard told him, the man did just so, and indeed he was able to ride about on the clouds. He traveled the world in this fashion, and brought back a map which he had drawn of the whole world both of men and of gods. Arriving back at the peak of the mountain in Ainu-land, he stepped off the cloud on to the mountain and descended down into the valley, told the wizard about his success and thanked him for the opportunity kindly granted to him whereby he could see the marvelous things, wonderful and strange.

The wizard was astonished. For what he had told the other man was a lie, a wicked lie invented with the sole intention of causing his death; for he hated him. Nevertheless, seeing that what he had simply meant for an idle tale was apparently an actual fact, he decided to see the world for himself in this easy way. So ascending the mountain-peak, and seeing a belt of clouds a short way below, he jumped off on to it, but fell into the valley below and died instantly.

That night the lord of the mountain appeared to the good man in a dream, and said: "The wizard has met his death, which his fraud and folly deserved. You I kept alive because you are a good man. So when, obedient to the wizard's advice, you leap off on to the cloud, I held you up, and showed you the world in order to make you a wiser man. Let all men learn from this how wickedness leads to condign punishment!"

The Yi Jing Apocrypha of Genghis Khan

The Land of the Shamuzi-Women

In ancient times, an Ainu chieftain of Iwanai went to sea with his two sons to catch sea-lions. They speared one sea-lion, which swam off with the spear still stuck in its body. Meanwhile, a strong wind began to blow down from the mountains. The men cut the rope which was tied to the spear. Then their boat floated on. Shortly after, they reached a beautiful land. Arriving near the shore, a number of women in fine garments came down from the mountains to the shore. They came down carrying a beautiful woman in a strange seat. Then all the woman who had come to the shore returned to the mountains. Only the woman in the strange seat came close to the boat and spoke to the men, saying: "This is the land of Shamuzi-women. It is a land where no men live. It is now spring, and there is something peculiar to this country of mine, you shall be taken care of in my house until autumn. In the winter, you shall become our husbands. The following spring I will send you home. Come with me."

The Ainu chief and his two sons did follow the woman in the strange seat into the mountains. They saw that the country was like a moorland. Then the Shamuzi entered the house. There was a room with a golden netting, like a mosquito-net. The three men were placed inside of it. The Shamuzi fed them. During the day, many women came in and sat beside the golden mosquito-net, watching the men. At nightfall they went home. Eventually autumn arrived. Then the Shamuzi spoke to the Ainu chief, saying: "As the fall of the leaf has now come, and as there are two vice-Shamuzies besides me, I will send your two sons to them. You yourself shall be my husband. Then two beautiful women came in, and led off the two sons by the hand, while the Shamuzi kept the chief for herself.

So it was that the men did stay with the Shamuzies. When spring came, the Ainu chieftain's wife spoke thus to him: "We women of this country are different from your land. When the grass begins to sprout, teeth sprout in our vaginas. Our husbands cannot stay with us. The east wind is our husband. When the east wind blows, we all turn our buttocks towards it and conceive children. Sometimes we bear male children. But these male children are killed and done away with when they become fit to lie with women. For that reason, this is a land for the Shamuzi only. It is called Shamuzi-land. So when you were brought by some bad god, you came to this land of mine, there were teeth in my vagina because it was summer, for which reason I did not marry you. But I married you when the teeth fell out. Now, as the teeth are again sprouting in my vagina because spring has come, it is now impossible for us to sleep together. I will send you home tomorrow. So do tell your sons to come here today in order to be ready."

The sons came. The Shamuzi stayed in the house. Then, with tears streaming down her face, she spoke thus: "Though it is dangerous, tonight is our last night. Let us sleep together!" Then the man, being much afraid, took a beautiful sheath for a knife in a bag in his bosom, and lay with the woman with this sheath. The mark of the teeth remained on the leather sheath. The next day dawned. Then the man went to his boat, taking his sons with him. The Shamuzi wept and spoke thus: "As a fair wind is blowing away from my country, you, if you set sail and sail straight ahead, will be able to reach your home at Iwanai." So then the men entered their boat, and went out to sea. A fair wind was blowing down from the mountains, and they went along under sail. After a time they saw land; they saw the mountains about Iwanai. Going on for a time, they came to the shore of Iwanai. Their wives were wearing widows' caps. So their husbands embraced them. So the story of Shamuzi-land was listened to carefully. All the Ainus saw the beautiful sheath which the chief had used with that woman.

The Book of Nyarzir

Know that the Powers of the Hexagram can be called once one has ventured forth into the regions of Nyarzir and has crossed each trigram in the space of one moon. Nyarzir was spoken about in the societies of man as Mount Nizir. And the Opening of the Sea must occur, the Soul of Fire prayer shall be performed, the Calling of the Shamuzi invoked And the Ninzuwu must be petitioned along with the Fire of Wutzki invoked.

After the rites of Opening the Temple have been performed, the Ninzuwu can now call the Hexagram by its name along with the Vasuh mantra that accompanies such. However, the Ninzuwu will find that at many times these signs will come to them in Dreams and after the Rites of the Celestial Gate. This rite can occur to one's on choosing, but was honored by the Warrior-Priests of Old during the New Moon, upon which the Prayer of Heaven must be performed, but only after the Opening of the Sea has occurred, and the Soul of Fire prayer has been invoked. Then the Call of the Shamuzi, and the unseen Ninzuwu, but not the Fire of Wutzki, for the Prayer of Heaven is the Fire of Heaven, and Johuta will teach thee this. These are said thrice:

The Yi Jing Apocrypha of Genghis Khan

Prayer of Heaven

Taka ama hari ni Kamu zumari masu Kamurogi
Kamuromi no Mikoto moshite
Sumemi oya Kamu Izanagi no Ohkami Tsukushi no
Himuka no Tachibana no
Odo no Awagigahara ni Misogi harae tamaishi Toki ne
are maser u
Harae do no Ohkami tachi Moromoro no Maga goto
Tsumi kegare o
Harae tamae Kiyome tamae to Maosu kotono Yoshi o
Amatsu kami Kunitsu kami Yao yorozu no Kami tachi
tomo ni Kikoshi mese to
Kashi komi Kashi komi mo mao su

Know that the aroma of fresh pine is good for the
Ceremonies of the Celestial Gate. These things are to take
place in the Light of the Sun. after the Prayer of Heaven
has been recited three times. After these things take
place Open the Celestial Gate. It is a rite only known by
those anointed by the Black Dragon And each dimension
must be called three times:

The Opening of the Celestial Gate

Izanagi-no-Mikoto, Izanami-no-Mikoto Mamori Tamae
Sakihae Tamae
Omo-Daru-no-Mikoto, Kashiko-ne-no-Mikoto, Mamori
Tamae Sakihae Tamae
Otonoji-no-Mikoto, Otomabe-no-Mikoto, Mamori Tamae
Sakihae Tamae
Uhijini-no-Mikoto, Suhijini-no-Mikoto Mamori Tamae
Sakihae Tamae
Toyo-kumo-nu-no-Mikoto Mamori Tamae Sakihae
Tamae
Kuni-no-satsuchi-no-Mikoto Mamori Tamae Sakihae
Tamae

Kuni-no-tokotachi-no-Mikoto Mamori Tamae Sakihae
Tamae

The Sign of Nyarzir

Nyarzir - The Cult of Mt. Nizir

"And the Bride of Nyarzir has the body of a beautiful woman wearing a white dress without legs. The head is that of four faces. The face of the North appears a Woman of Age and is made of Lapis Lazuli. The Face of the East is that of a Virgin and is made of Diamonds. The Face of the South is that of a Child and is made of the finest Gold. The Face of the West is that of a Mother and is made of Onyx."

The Bride of Nyarzir means Ichirei Shikon

Kushi-mitama: The Face of the West is that of a Mother and is made of Onyx.

Saki-mitama: The Face of the East is that of a Virgin and is made of Diamonds.

Ari-mitama: The Face of the South is that of a Child and is made of the finest Gold

The Yi Jing Apocrypha of Genghis Khan

Nigi-mitama: The Face of the North appears as a
Woman of Age and is made of Lapis Lazuli.

Johuta the Crow = Reikon

"The following are the Nine Books of Xuz, who some men call the Dehfu, Books of Life. It is only by proper use of this language can one access the realms of knowing. Take these words with caution."

(Lewhu)
Izanagi-no-Mikoto, Izanami-no-Mikoto

(Nzu)
Omo-Daru-no-Mikoto, Kashiko-ne-no-Mikoto

(Phe)
Otonoji-no-Mikoto, Otomabe-no-Mikoto

(Bnhu)
Uhijini-no-Mikoto, Suhijini-no-Mikoto

(Hmu)
Toyo-kumo-nu-no-Mikoto

(Tuu)
Kuni-no-satsuchi-no-Mikoto

(Aum)
Kuni-no-tokotachi-no-Mikoto Mamori

(Zhee)
Takamagahara

THE RITUAL FOR EVIL SPIRITS

I (your name), declare: When by the word of the progenitor and progenitrix, who divinely remaining in the plain of high Heaven, deigned to make the beginning of things, they divinely deigned to assemble the many hundred myriads of gods in the high city of Heaven, and deigned divinely to take counsel in council, saying: "When we cause our Sovereign Grandchild's augustness, to leave Heaven's eternal seat, to cleave a path with might through Heaven's manifold clouds, and to descend from Heaven, with orders tranquilly to rule the country of fresh spikes, which flourishes in the midst of the reed-moor as a peaceful country, what god shall we send first to divinely sweep away, sweep away and subdue the gods who are turbulent in the country of fresh spikes "; all the gods pondered and declared: "You shall send Amenohohi's augustness, and subdue them," declared they. Wherefore they sent him down from Heaven, but he did not declare an answer; and having next sent Takemikuma's augustness, he also, obeying his father's words, did not declare an answer. Ame-no-waka-hiko also, whom they sent, did not declare an answer, but immediately perished by the calamity of a bird on high. Wherefore they pondered afresh by the word of the Heavenly gods, and having deigned to send down from Heaven the two pillars of gods, Futsunushi and Takemika-dzuchi's augustness, who having deigned divinely to sweep away, and sweep away, and deigned divinely to soften, and soften the gods who were turbulent, and silenced the rocks, trees, and the least leaf of herbs likewise that had spoken, they caused the Sovereign Grandchild's augustness to descend from Heaven.

I fulfil your praises, saying: As to the Offerings set up, so that the sovereign gods who come into the heavenly house of the Sovereign Grandchild's augustness, which, after he had fixed upon as a peaceful country - the country of great Yamato where the sun is high, as the center of the countries of the four quarters bestowed upon him when he was thus sent down from Heaven - stoutly planting the house-pillars on the bottom-most rocks, and exalting the cross-beams to the plain of high Heaven, the builders had made for his shade from the Heavens and shade from the sun, and wherein he will tranquilly rule the country as a peaceful country may, without deigning to be turbulent, deigning to be fierce, and deigning to hurt, knowing, by virtue of their divinity, the things which were begun in the plain of high Heaven, deigning to correct with Divine-correcting and Great-correcting, remove hence out to the clean places of the mountain streams which look far away over the four quarters, and rule them as their own place. Let the sovereign gods tranquilly take with clear hearts, as peaceful offerings and sufficient offerings the great offerings which I set up, piling them upon the tables like a range of hills, providing bright cloth, glittering cloth, soft cloth, and coarse cloth, as a thing to see plain in - a mirror: as things to play with-beads: as things to shoot off with - a bow and arrows: as things to strike and cut with - a

sword: as a thing which gallops out - a horse; as to liquor
- raising high the beer-jars, filling and ranging in rows
the bellies of the beer-jars, with grains of rice and ears;
as to the things which dwell in the hills things soft of
hair, and things rough of hair; as to the things which
grow in the great field plain - sweet herbs and bitter
herbs; as to the things which dwell in the blue sea plain
things broad of fin and things narrow of fin, down to
weeds of the offing and weeds of the short, and without
deigning to be turbulent, deigning to be fierce, and
deigning to hurt, remove out to the wide and clean places
of the mountain streams, and by virtue of their divinity
be tranquil.

THE HARVEST RITUAL

I declare in the presence of the sovereign gods of the
Harvest, If the sovereign gods will bestow, in many-
bundled spikes and in luxuriant spikes, the late-ripening
harvest which they will bestow, the late-ripening harvest
which will be produced by the dripping of foam from the
arms, and by drawing the mud together between the
opposing thighs, then I will fulfil their praises by
presenting the first-fruits in a thousand ears, and in
many hundred ears; raising high the beer-jars, filling
and ranging in rows the bellies of the beer-jars, I will
present them in juice and in grain. As to things which
grow in the great field plain - sweet herbs and bitter
herbs; as to things which dwell in the blue sea plain
things wide of fin, and things narrow of fin, down to the
weeds of the offing, and weeds of the shore; and as to
Clothes, with bright cloth, glittering cloth, soft cloth,
and coarse cloth will I fulfil their praises. And having
furnished a white horse, a white boar, and a white cock,
and the various kinds of things in the presence of the
sovereign gods of the Harvest, I fulfil their praises by

presenting the great Offerings of the sovereign Grand-
child's augustness.

THE RITUAL FOR THE WIND-GODS

I declare in the presence of the sovereign gods, whose praises are fulfilled at Tatsuta. Because they had not allowed, firstly the five sorts of grain which the Sovereign Grand-child's augustness, who ruled the great country of many islands at Shikishima, took with ruddy countenance as his long and lasting food, and the things produced by the people, down to the least leaf of the herbs, to ripen, and had spoilt them not for one year, or for two years, but for continuous years, he deigned to command: "As to the Heart of the god which shall come forth in the divinings of all the men who are learned in things, declare what god it is."

Whereupon the men learned in things divined with their divinings, but they declared that no Heart of a god appears.

When he had heard this, the Sovereign Grand-child's augustness deigned to conjure them, saying: "I sought to fulfil their praises as heavenly temples and country temples, without forgetting or omitting, and have so acted, but let the god, whatever god he be, that has prevented the things produced by the people of the region under Heaven from ripening, and has spoilt them, make known his Heart."

Hereupon they made the Sovereign Grand-child's augustness to know in a great dream, and made him to know their names, saying:

"Our names, who have prevented the things made by the people of the region under Heaven from ripening and have spoilt them, by visiting them with bad winds and rough waters, are Heaven's Pillars augustness and Country's Pillars augustness." And they made him to know, saying: "If for the Offerings which shall be set up in our presence there be furnished various sorts of Offerings, as to Clothes, bright cloth, glittering cloth, soft cloth, and coarse cloth, and the five kinds of things, a shield, a spear, and a horse furnished with a saddle; if our house be fixed at Wonu, in Tachinu, at Tatsuta, in a place where the morning sun is opposite, and the evening sun is hidden, and praises be fulfilled in our presence, we will bless and ripen the things produced by the people of the region under Heaven, firstly the five sorts of grain, down to the least leaf of the herbs."

Therefore hear, all ye wardens and vergers, by declaring in the presence of the sovereign gods that, having fixed the House-pillars in the place which the sovereign gods had taught by words and made known, in order to fulfil praises in the presence of the sovereign gods, the Sovereign Grandchild's augustness has caused his great Offerings to be lifted up and brought, and has fulfilled their praises, sending the princes and counselors as his messengers

THE FIRE RITUAL

I declare with the great ritual, the Heavenly ritual, which was bestowed on him at the time when, by the Word of the Sovereign's dear progenitor and progenitrix, who divinely remain in the plain of high Heaven, they bestowed on him the region under Heaven, saying: "Let the Sovereign Grandchild's augustness tranquilly rule over the country of fresh spikes which flourishes in the midst of the reed-moor, as a peaceful region."

When the two pillars, the divine Izanagi and Izanami's augustness, younger sister and elder brother, had intercourse, and she had deigned to bear the many tens of countries of the countries, and the many tens of islands of the islands, and had deigned to bear the many hundred myriads of gods, she also deigned to bear her dear youngest child of all, the Fire-producer god, and her hidden parts being burnt, she bid in the rocks, and said: "My dear elder brother's augustness, deign not to look upon me for seven nights of nights and seven days of sunshine"; but when, before the seven days were fulfilled, he looked, thinking her remaining hidden to be strange, she deigned to say: "My hidden parts were burnt when I bore fire." At such a time I said, "My dear elder brother's augustness, deign not to look upon me, but you violently looked upon me "; and after saying, "My dear elder brother's augustness shall rule the upper country; I will rule the lower country," she deigned to hide in the rocks, and having come to the flat hill of darkness, she thought and said: "I have come hither, having born and left a bad-hearted child in the upper country, ruled over by my illustrious elder brother's augustness," and going back she bore other children. Having born the Water-goddess, the gourd, the river-weed, and the clay-hill maiden, four sorts of things, she taught them with words, and made them to know, saying: "If the heart of this bad-hearted child becomes violent, let the Water-goddess take the gourd, and the clay-hill maiden take the river-weed, and pacify him."

In consequence of this I fulfil his praises, and say that for the things set up, so that he may deign not to be awfully quick of heart in their great place of the Sovereign Grandchild's augustness, there are provided bright cloth, glittering cloth, soft cloth, and coarse cloth, and the five kinds of things; as to things which dwell in the blue sea plain, there are things wide of fin and things narrow of fin, down to the weeds of the offing and weeds of the shore; as to liquor, raising high the beer-jars, filling and ranging in rows the bellies of the beer-jars, piling the offerings up, even to rice in grain and rice in ear, like a range of hills, I fulfil his praises with the great ritual, the heavenly ritual.

RITUALS TO THE SUN-GODDESS

*Know that the name Amaterasu-Omikami is the greatest protection. It is worth well if said eleven times

He (the priest envoy) says: "Hear all of you, ministers of the gods and sanctifiers of offerings, the great ritual, the Heavenly ritual, declared in the great presence of the From-Heaven-shining-great deity, whose praises are fulfilled by setting up the stout pillars of the great house, and exalting the cross-beam to the plain of high Heaven at the sources of the Isuzu river at Udji in Watarahi."

He says: "It is the Sovereign's great Word. Hear all of you, ministers of the gods and sanctifiers of offerings, the fulfilling of praises on this seventeenth day of the sixth moon of this year, as the morning sun goes up in glory, of the Oho-Nakatomi, who-having abundantly piled up like a range of hills the tribute thread and sanctified liquor and food presented as of usage by the people of the deity's houses attributed to her in the three departments and in various countries and places, so that she deign to bless his (the Mikado's) life as a long life and his age as a luxuriant age eternally and unchangingly as multitudinous piles of rock; may deign to bless the children who are born to him, and deigning to cause to flourish the five kinds of grain which the men of - a hundred functions and the peasants of the countries in the four quarters of the region under Heaven long and peacefully cultivate and eat, and guarding and benefiting them deign to bless them - is hidden by the great offering-wands."

I declare in the great presence of the From-Heaven-shining-great deity who sits in Ise. Because the Sovereign great goddess bestows on him the countries of the four quarters over which her glance extends, as far as the limit where Heaven stands up like a wall, as far as the bounds where the country stands up distant, as far as the limit where the blue clouds spread flat, as far as the bounds where the white clouds lie away fallen-the blue sea plain as far as the limit whither come the prows of the ships without drying poles or paddles, the ships which continuously crowd on the great sea plain, and the roads which men travel by land, as far as the limit whither come the horses' hoofs, with the baggage-cords tied tightly, treading the uneven rocks and tree-roots and standing up continuously in a long path without a break - making the narrow countries wide and the hilly countries plain, and as it were drawing together the distant countries by throwing many tens of ropes over them - he will pile up the first-fruits like a range of hills in the great presence of the Sovereign great goddess, and will peacefully enjoy the remainder.

Use of the Tide Jewels

Now the map of the trigram is the road that one must take to perfect thy soul. It is a sacred path, and the eight keys for the city in Heaven.

The formula for obtaining such is not like the men of the nations, but in the Soul of Fire Prayer. And when there is hesitation in moving from one letter to the next, it is a yin lin. When there is no hesitation when moving from one letter to the next, it is a yang line. This is how the Tide Jewels are used.

Ryohei Uchida, Founder of the Black Dragon Society, Meeting With Mikao Usui (1925)

Recently, I had the opportunity to speak with Dr. Mikao Usui and to discuss with him the practice of Reiki and the future of Japan.

I am certain that Dr. Usui's discovery of this healing art is inspired by the gods. After meeting with him, I am convinced that this practice of Reiki is the practice of Shinto. The principles are Shinto, as Shinto is not a religion, but an emotion, and the preservation of such, will lead to the advancement of humanity throughout the globe.

The Yi Jing Apocrypha of Genghis Khan

The connection between Shinto and Reiki can be clearly seen in its symbol for the tell a story that was told during the Age of the Gods. The symbols of Dr. Usui's system come from Shinto mythology.

Dai Ko Myo: represents Izanagi-no-Mikoto and Izanami-no-Mikoto. These two forces produced the nest three. Certainly, Izanagi-no-Mikoto is the Master and the one who was a gatekeeper. This first child they had together was Amatereasu-Ohmikami.

Hon-Sha-Ze-Sho-Nen is Amaterasu-Omikami, the first child of Izanagi-no-Mikoto and Izanami-no-Mikoto. When she was born, her radiance was so bright that her parents sent her to heaven. The sun's ray reach everywhere on earth.

Sei-He-Ki: The next child by Izanagi-no-Mikoto and Izanami-no-Mikoto was the ruler of the moon, Tsukiyomi-no-Mikoto. It is said that he shares a similar nature as his sister Amaterasu-Omikami, but rules the emotions.

Cho Ku Rei: Susanoo-no-Mikoto was the next child ny Izanagi-no-Mikoto and Izanami-no-Mikoto and was said to rule the earth and the sea.

Dr. Usui's work is promoting the way of Japan. I will support him in his endeavors. It is possible that his work may lead to the elixir of life.

The Yi Jing Apocrypha of Genghis Khan

THE BLACK DRAGON SOCIETY MEMORANDUM

(Published on October 29th 1914. An esoteric document with special meaning for the Yi Jing Sorcerer.))

PART I. THE EUROPEAN WAR AND THE CHINESE QUESTION

The present gigantic struggle in Europe has no parallel in history. Not only will the equilibrium of Europe be affected and its effect felt all over the globe, but its results will create a New Era in the political and social world. Therefore, whether or not the Imperial Japanese Government can settle the Far Eastern Question and bring to realization our great Imperial policy depends on our being able to skilfully avail ourselves of the world's general trend of affairs so as to extend our influence and to decide upon a course of action towards China which shall be practical in execution. If our authorities and people view the present European War with indifference and without deep concern, merely devoting their attention to the attack on Kiaochow, neglecting the larger issues of the war, they will have brought to naught our great Imperial policy, and committed a blunder greater than which it cannot be conceived. We are constrained to submit this statement of policy for the consideration of our authorities, not because we are fond of argument but because we are deeply anxious for our national welfare.

No one at present can foretell the outcome of the European War. If the Allies meet with reverses and victory shall crown the arms of the Germans and

258

Austrians, German militarism will undoubtedly dominate the European Continent and extend southward and eastward to other parts of the world. Should such a state of affairs happen to take place the consequences resulting therefrom will be indeed great and extensive. On this account we must devote our most serious attention to the subject. If, on the other hand, the Germans and Austrians should be crushed by the Allies, Germany will be deprived of her present status as a Federated State under a Kaiser. The Federation will be disintegrated into separate states and Prussia will have to be content with the status of a second-rate Power. Austria and Hungary, on account of this defeat, will consequently be divided. What their final fate will be, no one would now venture to predict. In the meantime Russia will annex Galicia and the Austrian Poland; France will repossess Alsace and Lorraine; Great Britain will occupy the German Colonies in Africa and the South Pacific: Servia and Montenegro will take Bosnia, Herzegovina and a certain portion of Austrian territory; thus making such great changes in the map of Europe that even the Napoleonic War in 1815 could not find a parallel.

When these events take place, not only will Europe experience great changes, but we should not ignore the fact that they will occur also in China and in the South Pacific. After Russia has replaced Germany in the territories lost by Germany and Austria, she will hold a controlling influence in Europe, and, for a long time to come, will have nothing to fear from her western frontier. Immediately after the war she will make an effort to carry out her policy of expansion in the East and will not relax her effort until she has acquired a controlling influence in China. At the same time, Great Britain will strengthen her position in the Yangtze Valley and prohibit any other country from getting a footing there. France will do likewise in Yunnan province, using it as her base of operations for further encroachments upon China and never hesitate to extend her advantages. We must therefore seriously study the situation, remembering always that the combined action of Great Britain, Russia and France will not only affect Europe but that we can even foresee that it will also affect China.

Whether this combined action on the part of England, France and Russia is to terminate at the end of the war or to continue to operate, we cannot now predict. But after peace in Europe is restored, these Powers will certainly turn their attention to the expansion of their several spheres of interest in China, and, in the adjustment, their interests will most likely conflict with one another. If their interests do not conflict, they will work jointly to solve the Chinese Question. On this point we have not the least doubt. If England, France and Russia are actually to combine for the coercion of China, what course is to be adopted by the Imperial Japanese Government to meet the situation? What proper means shall we employ to maintain our influence and extend our interests within this ring of rivalry and competition? It is necessary that we bear in mind the final results of the European War and forestall the trend of events succeeding it so as to be able to decide upon a policy towards China and determine the action to be ultimately taken. If we remain passive, the Imperial Japanese Government's policy towards China will lose that subjective influence and our diplomacy will be checked forever by the combined force of the other Powers. The peace of the Far East will be thus endangered and even the existence of the Japanese Empire as a nation will no doubt be imperiled. It is therefore our first important duty at this moment to enquire of our Government what course is to be adopted to face that general situation after the war. What preparations are being made to meet the combined pressure of the Allies upon China? What policy has been followed to solve the Chinese Question? When the European War is terminated and peace restored we are not concerned so much with the question whether it be the Dual Monarchies or the Triple Entente which emerge victorious, but whether, in anticipation of the future expansion of European influence in the Continents of Europe and Asia, the Imperial Japanese Government should or should not hesitate to employ force to check the movement before this occurrence. Now is the most opportune moment for Japan to quickly solve the Chinese Question. Such, an opportunity will not occur for hundreds of years to come. Not only is it Japan's divine duty to act now, but present conditions in China favor the execution of such a plan. We should by all means decide and act at once. If our authorities do not avail themselves of this rare opportunity, great duty will surely be encountered in future in the settlement of this Chinese question. Japan will be isolated from the European Powers after the war, and will be regarded by them with envy and jealousy just as Germany is now regarded. Is it not then a vital necessity for Japan to solve at this very moment the Chinese Question?

PART II. THE CHINESE QUESTION AND THE DEFENSIVE ALLIANCE

It is a very important matter of policy whether the Japanese Government, in obedience to its divine mission, shall solve the Chinese Question in a heroic manner by making China voluntarily rely upon Japan. To force China to such a position there is nothing else for the Imperial Japanese Government to do but to take advantage of the present opportunity to seize the reins of political and financial power and to enter by all means into a defensive alliance with her under secret terms as enumerated below:

The Secret Terms of the Defensive Alliance

The Imperial Japanese Government, with due respect for the Sovereignty and Integrity of China and with the object and hope of maintaining the peace of the Far East, undertakes to share the responsibility of co-operating with China to guard her against internal trouble and foreign invasion and China shall accord to

Japan special facilities in the matter of China's National Defense, or the protection of Japan's special rights and privileges and for these objects the following treaty of Alliance is to be entered into between the two contracting parties:

1. When there is internal trouble in China or when she is at war with another nation or nations, Japan shall send her army to render assistance, to assume the responsibility of guarding Chinese territory and to maintain peace and order in China.

2. China agrees to recognize Japan's privileged position in South Manchuria and Inner Mongolia and to cede the sovereign rights of these regions to Japan to enable her to carry out a scheme of local defence on a permanent basis.

3. After the Japanese occupation of Kiaochow, Japan shall acquire all the rights and privileges heretofore enjoyed by the Germans in regard to railways, mines and all other interests, and after peace and order is restored in Tsingtao, the place shall be handed back to China to be opened as an International Treaty port.

4. For the maritime defence of China and Japan, China shall lease strategic harbors along the coast of the Fukien province to Japan to be converted into naval bases and grant to Japan in the said province all railway and mining rights.

5. For the reorganization of the Chinese army China shall entrust the training and drilling of the army to Japan.

6. For the unification of China's firearms and munitions of war, China shall adopt firearms of Japanese pattern, and at the same time establish arsenals (with the help of Japan) in different strategic points.

7. With the object of creating and maintaining a Chinese Navy, China shall entrust the training of her navy to Japan.

8. With the object of reorganizing her finances and improving the methods of taxation, China shall entrust the work to Japan, and the latter shall elect competent financial experts who shall act as first-class advisers to the Chinese Government.

9. China shall engage Japanese educational experts as educational advisers and extensively establish schools in different parts of the country to teach Japanese so as to raise the educational standard of the country.

10. China shall first consult with and obtain the consent of Japan before she can enter into an agreement with another Power for making loans, the leasing of territory, or the cession of the same.

From the date of the signing of this Defensive Alliance, Japan and China shall work together hand-in-hand. Japan will assume the responsibility of safeguarding Chinese territory and maintaining the peace and order in China. This will relieve China of all future anxieties and enable her to proceed energetically with her reforms, and, with a sense of territorial security, she may wait for her national development and regeneration. Even after the present European War is over and peace is restored China will absolutely have nothing to fear in the future of having pressure brought against her by the foreign powers. It is only thus that permanent peace can be secured in the Far East.

But before concluding this Defensive Alliance, two points must first be ascertained and settled. (1) Its bearing on the Chinese Government. (2) Its bearing on those Powers having intimate relations with, and great interests in, China.

In considering its effect on the Chinese Government, Japan must try to foresee whether the position of China's present ruler Yuan Shih-kai shall be permanent or not; whether the present Government's policy will enjoy the confidence of a large section of the Chinese people; whether Yuan Shih-kai will readily agree to the

Japanese Government's proposal to enter into a treaty of alliance with us. These are points to which we are bound to give a thorough consideration. Judging by the attitude hitherto adopted by Yuan Shih-kai we know he has always resorted to the policy of expediency in his diplomatic dealings, and although he may outwardly show friendliness towards us, he will in fact rely upon the influence of the different Powers as the easiest check against us and refuse to accede to our demands. Take for a single instance, his conduct towards us since the Imperial Government declared war against Germany and his action will then be clear to all. Whether we can rely upon the ordinary friendly methods of diplomacy to gain our object or not it does not require much wisdom to decide. After the gigantic struggle in Europe is over, leaving aside America, which will not press for advantage, China will not be able to obtain any loans from the other Powers. With a depleted treasury, without means to pay the officials and the army, with local bandits inciting the poverty-stricken populace to trouble, with the revolutionists waiting for opportunities to rise, should an insurrection actually occur while no outside assistance can be rendered to quell it we are certain it will be impossible for Yuan Shih-kai, single-handed, to restore order and consolidate the country. The result will be that the nation will be cut up into many parts beyond all hope of remedy. That this state of affairs will come is not difficult to foresee. When this occurs, shall we uphold Yuan's Government and assist him to suppress the internal insurrection with the certain assurance that we could influence him to agree to our demands, or shall we help the revolutionists to achieve a success and realize our object through them? This question must be definitely decided upon this very moment so that we may put it into practical execution. If we do not look into the future fate of China but go blindly to uphold Yuan's Government, to enter into a Defensive Alliance with China, hoping thus to secure a complete realization of our object by assisting him to suppress the revolutionists, it is obviously a wrong policy. Why? Because the majority of the Chinese people have lost all faith in the tottering Yuan Shih-kai who is discredited and attacked by the whole nation for having sold his country. If Japan gives Yuan the support, his Government, though in a very precarious state, may possibly avoid destruction. Yuan Shih-kai belongs to that school of politicians who are fond of employing craftiness and cunning. He may be friendly to us for a time, but he will certainly abandon us and again befriend the other Powers when the European war is at an end. Judging by his past we have no doubt as to what he will do in the future. For Japan to ignore the general sentiment of the Chinese people and support Yuan Shih-kai with the hope that we can settle with him the Chinese Question is a blunder indeed. Therefore, in order to secure the permanent peace of the Far East, instead of supporting a Chinese Government which can neither be long continued in power nor assist in the attainment of our object, we should rather support the 400,000,000 Chinese people to renovate their corrupt Government, to change its present form, to maintain peace and order in the land and to usher into China a new era of prosperity so that China and Japan may in fact as well as in name be brought into the most intimate and vital relations with each other. China's era of prosperity is based on the Chino-Japanese Alliance and this Alliance is the foundational power for the repelling of the foreign aggression that is to be directed against the Far East at the conclusion of the European War. This Alliance is also the foundation-stone of the peace of the world. Japan therefore should take this as the last warning and immediately solve this question. Since the Imperial Japanese Government has considered it imperative to support the Chinese people, we should induce the Chinese revolutionists, the Imperialists and other Chinese malcontents to create trouble all over China. The whole country will be thrown into disorder and Yuan's Government will consequently be overthrown. We shall then select a man from amongst the most influential and most noted of the 400,000,000 of Chinese and help him to organize a new form of Government and to consolidate the whole country. In the meantime our army must assist in the restoration of peace and order in the country, and in the protection of the lives and properties of the people, so that they may gladly tender their allegiance to the new Government which will then naturally confide in and rely upon Japan. It is after the accomplishment of only these things that we shall without difficulty gain our object by the conclusion of a Defensive Alliance with China.

For us to incite the Chinese revolutionists and malcontents to rise in China we consider the present to be the most opportune moment. The reason why these men cannot now carry on an active campaign is because they are insufficiently provided with funds. If the Imperial Government can take advantage of this fact to make them a loan and instruct them to rise simultaneously, great commotion and disorder will surely prevail all over China. We can intervene and easily adjust matters.

The progress of the European War warns Japan with greater urgency of the imperative necessity of solving this most vital of questions. The Imperial Government cannot be considered as embarking on a rash project. This opportunity will not repeat itself for our benefit. We must avail ourselves of this chance and under no circumstances hesitate. Why should we wait for the spontaneous uprising of the revolutionists and malcontents? Why should we not think out and lay down a plan beforehand? When we examine into the form of government in China, we must ask whether the existing Republic is well suited to the national temperament and well adapted to the thoughts and aspirations of the Chinese people. From the time the Republic of China was established up to the present moment, if what it has passed through is to be compared to what it ought to be in the matter of administration and unification, we find disappointment everywhere. Even the revolutionists themselves, the very ones who first advocated the Republican form of government, acknowledge that they have made a mistake. The retention of the Republican form of Government in China will be a great future obstacle in the way of a Chino-Japanese alliance. And why must it be so? Because in a Republic the fundamental principles of government as well as the social and moral aims of the people are distinctly different from that of a Constitutional Monarchy. Their laws and administration also conflict. If Japan act as a guide to China and China model herself after Japan, it will only then be possible for the two nations to solve by mutual effort the Far East Question without differences and disagreements. Therefore, to start from the foundation for the purpose of reconstructing the Chinese Government, of establishing a Chino-Japanese Alliance, of maintaining the permanent peace of the Far East and of realizing the consummation of Japan's Imperial policy, we must take advantage of the present opportunity to alter China's Republican form of Government into a Constitutional Monarchy which shall necessarily be identical, in all its details, to the Constitutional Monarchy of Japan, and to no other. This is really the key and first principle to be firmly held for the actual reconstruction of the form of Government in China. If China changes her Republican form of Government to that of a Constitutional Monarchy, shall we, in the selection of a new ruler, restore the Emperor Hsuan T'ung to his throne or choose the most capable man from the Monarchists or select the most worthy member from among the revolutionists? We think, however, that it is advisable at present to leave this question to the exigency of the future when the matter is brought up for decision. But we must not lose sight of the fact that to actually put into execution this policy of a Chino-Japanese Alliance and the transformation of the Republic of China into a Constitutional Monarchy, is, in reality, the fundamental principle to be adopted for the reconstruction of China.

We shall now consider the bearing of this Defensive Alliance on the other Powers. Needless to say, Japan and China will in no way impair the rights and interests already acquired by the Powers. At this moment it is of paramount importance for Japan to come to a special understanding with Russia to define our respective spheres in Manchuria and Mongolia so that the two countries may co-operate with each other in the future. This means that Japan after the acquisition of sovereign rights in South Manchuria and Inner Mongolia will work together with Russia after her acquisition of sovereign rights in North Manchuria and Outer Mongolia to maintain the status quo, and endeavour by every effort to protect the peace of the Far East. Russia, since the outbreak of the European War, has not only laid aside all ill-feelings against Japan, but has adopted the same attitude as her Allies and shown warm friendship for us. No matter how we regard the Manchurian and Mongolian Questions in the future she is anxious that we find some way of settlement. Therefore we need not doubt but that Russia, in her attitude towards this Chinese Question, will be able to come to an understanding with us for mutual co-operation.

The British sphere of influence and interest in China is cantered in Tibet and the Yangtsze Valley. Therefore, if Japan can come to some satisfactory arrangement with China in regard to Tibet and also give certain privileges to Great Britain in the Yangtze Valley, with an assurance to protect those privileges, no matter how powerful Great Britain might be, she will surely not oppose Japan's policy in regard to this Chinese Question. While this present European War is going on Great Britain has never asked Japan to render her assistance. That her strength will certainly not enable her to oppose us in the future need not be doubted in the least.

The Yi Jing Apocrypha of Genghis Khan

Since Great Britain and Russia will not oppose Japan's policy towards China, it can readily be seen what attitude France will adopt in regard to the subject. What Japan must now somewhat reckon with is America. But America in her attitude towards us regarding our policy towards China has already declared the principle of maintaining China's territorial integrity and equal opportunity and will be satisfied, if we do not impair America's already acquired rights and privileges. We think America will also have no cause for complaint. Nevertheless America has in the East a naval force which can be fairly relied upon, though not sufficiently strong to be feared. Therefore in Japan's attitude towards America there is nothing really for us to be afraid of.

Since China's condition is such on the one hand and the Powers' relation towards China is such on the other hand, Japan should avail herself in the meantime of the European War to definitely decide upon a policy towards China, the most important move being the transformation of the Chinese Government to be followed up by preparing for the conclusion of the Defensive Alliance. The precipitate action on the part of our present Cabinet in acceding to the request of Great Britain to declare war against Germany without having definitely settled our policy towards China has no real connection with our future negotiations with China or affects the political condition in the Far East. Consequently, all intelligent Japanese, of every walk of life throughout the land, are very deeply concerned about the matter.

Our Imperial Government should now definitely change our dependent foreign policy which is being directed by others into an independent foreign policy which shall direct others, proclaiming the same with solemn sincerity to the world and carrying it out with determination. If we do so, even the gods and spirits will give way. These are important points in our policy towards China and the result depends on how we carry them out. Can our authorities firmly make up their mind to solve this Chinese Question by the actual carrying out of this fundamental principle? If they show irresolution while we have this heaven-conferred chance and merely depend on the good will of the other Powers, we shall eventually have greater pressure to be brought against the Far East after the European War is over, when the present equilibrium will be destroyed. That day will then be too late for us to repent our folly. We are therefore impelled by force of circumstances to urge our authorities to a quicker sense of the situation and to come to a determination.

Appendix A: What Is Shinto?

Shinto is often described as the indigenous faith of the Japanese people. It is probably more correct to define Shinto as being the indigenous faith of the human race that has been preserved by the Japanese people.

Different than many religions of the world, Shinto has no founder and no body of sacred writings which its adherents must follow, and this aspect of Shinto reveals that it was the primordial faith of the human race. The idea of a religion having a founder and its practitioners must follow a set of "sacred" writings can only be defined as someone from an advanced civilization sharing its culture with an uncivilized people. Think about it for a second. Although religious mythology throughout the world may vary, there is one point that is consistent among these; all of the world's "prophets" that carried a "divine message" had to deliver such to an uncivilized people, or a nation that fell in disaccord with the way of heaven and earth.

Shinto reveals there was a time when man held the standard of its creator, following the ways of heaven and earth. It was a time of innocence, though concerns over the basic human needs and survival were always prominent in the mind of man from his beginning.

While it may be difficult for some to imagine the life of the human race during a time of such innocence, if we were to reflect on the basic aspects of life that preoccupied man during times of remote antiquity, the vision is easy to capture. Families worked as a unit to acquire food, shelter, and clothing. In such an environment, life was simple and egoless.

It was in this egoless state that the clarity of man's role in the universal scheme of things was easily seen. Human existence could not be possible if nature did not provide man with food, sustenance, and shelter. Based on such, it is evident that man was dependent on its primary parents, the Earth, the Sun, and other aspects of nature that life, and its sustaining qualities were all made possible. Following the *way of the gods*, is following the science of life. It was during the 6th century A.D., after Mahayana Buddhism had taken root in Japan, that this science of life was called Shinto in effort to distinguish this primordial faith from foreign spiritual practices that were gaining popularity in the Land of the Rising Sun.

The term Shinto is composed of two kanji, *"shin"* meaning *divine, gods, or spirits*, known as Kami, and *"to"* meaning *path of study, the way*, a derivative of the Chinese term *tao. The term Shinto was used to describe the practices of the indigenous people of Japan, and in some ways these practices resembled many of the rites practiced by Taoists who entered Japan from China. Taoism is another faith that borrowed much from the nature cults existing in China.* The Encyclopedia of

World Environmental History, Volume 3, by
Shepard Krech, states the following on page 1111:

**"Many scholars now believe that Japanese
actually borrowed the word "Shinto" from an
eighth-century Chinese word for Taoism...In the
eighth century, the Yamato state that Taoist
priests travel to Japan from China, and in time the
entire Japanese conception of empire and even
the cult of emperors themselves took on a Taoist
flavor. Nonetheless, early Japanese probably did
not identify, isolate, and categorize Shinto as
their "religion." Rather, for a people who lived
close to nature on a wild and mountAinuus
archipelago, Shinto probably constituted
everything they knew and sought to know about
the natural world."**

**Krech's observation confirms points presented in
our discussion. First, the indigenous practices that
relate to the nature cults of Japan, which were
later called Shinto, were not viewed as a
"religion" in the modern sense of the term, but
was in fact the science of life. Secondly, we learn
that *"Shinto probably constituted everything they
knew and sought to know about the natural
world."***

**Different than present-day opinions, it is modern
man who has regressed during recent times and
become primitive in his thinking. He is now a
terror to the very thing that sustains his life,
nature. His ego dictates that he is superior to the
very thing he needs to survive. The ego of modern
man has led him to categorize those who followed**

the *ways of the gods* as primitive. It is a sad state of affairs indeed, for he has lost his way and does not know how to communicate with the world around him, something that every living creature in nature can do. It is interesting to note that even in the insect world, there is a relationship between creatures of different kinds, plant life, and the heavenly bodies. Unfortunately, the ego of modern man has made it appear that the reverse is true, where the nature cults of old were not advanced in their knowledge and were primitive in thinking.

While the ego of modern man has led to the massive destruction of Earth's ecological system, he attempts to reinforce his egotistical views on the world by exalting the religions of the handicapped. A religion whose adherents believe in morbid concepts, like the creator of our entire universe requires a human sacrifice to forgive man, and still be considered a *god of love*. Another hypocritical belief is that the creator of our entire universe would actually command one nation to go out and kill every man, woman, and child, of an opposing nation in order to acquire some land. It is in the propagation of these so-called religious ideas that we find the plights of an egotistical sociopath accepted as the actions of an intelligent being. After establishing a spirit of disillusionment by spreading such morbid propaganda around the world, modern man then attempted to invalidate his own point of origin in an effort to appear superior. Today, we find this hypocrisy has finally spread to areas of academia as seen in the modern definition of Shinto itself.

Many Western sources have implied that Shinto began around 700 A.D. This is a ridiculous claim since we know that Shinto has no founder or sacred body of scriptures. If Shinto has no founder how can it be given a said date of origin? Efforts such as these clearly illustrate how propagators of various morbid systems of spirituality try to make their degrading theological views actual fact. It is a very sad thing indeed.

Shinto is the science of life. The indigenous people of Japan knew it as such, and incorporated in it are all aspects of life, including philosophy, religion, and science. Shinto is not a belief system, but the life you lead. There are many Japanese people who view religion as a system of control, or for the emotionally handicapped. It is due to such that many Japanese people will say they are atheists. This view does not make them less spiritual in their approach to life. But systems that appear separate from life are viewed as schemes to rob the spiritually malnourished. The fact that "Shinto" itself is not a religion, but a way of life, can be seen in its most scientific aspect, namely, the Kami.

Appendix B: The Kami

The heart of Shinto, or Japanese spirituality, cannot be captured if one lacks an understanding of the Kami. Kami is usually defined in the West, as the Japanese word for effigy, a principle and any supernatural being. While many attempts have been made by Western scholars to define the term *Kami*, it would be a grave error to compare such to the gods and spirits of Biblical mythology. This is not to say that it is wrong to define the term *kami* as gods, spirits, and sentient beings, but this perspective is quite different than how Christians revere Jesus Christ.

The term *kami* consist of two parts, *ka* meaning fire, and *mi* meaning water. Therefore, an accurate description of the term kami would be the alchemy of fire and water. Still, for the Western mind, and those outside the view of ancient Japanese thought, this in itself may not be clear definition.

The fire referred to in our discussion so far, is the radiating energy over a particular environment. For example, the appearance of a rose garden triggers a certain amount of emotional influence upon all other objects in that same environment. This radiating emotional energy is the *ka* or fire. The ka of an object can be suppressed or expanded based on the atmosphere it exists in. While the radiating force of a rose garden may thrive in a certain atmosphere, like a sunny day in the month of June, its influence would not be as strong during wintertime. The different atmospheric conditions play a large part in how much emotional energy any given object can radiate. These atmospheric conditions, or atmosphere, are symbolic of water or *mi*. In a previous work entitled, *The Dark Knight of Nyarlathotep*, we find the following under the chapter *True Religion*:

"In the so-called modern world, terms like polytheism seem to denote some sort of primitive form of spirituality, when in fact, it was a synthesis of how to define the subtle energy that permeates throughout all objects and animates all living things. So in ancient times, a body of water, or an ocean, was considered to be a deity. Now the fact that this ocean was considered to be a deity should not be interpreted in the same manner of how Christians worship Jesus, but as a force of influence upon the environment. Other objects of nature were also deified based on their influence over the environment. These forces were scientifically categorized based on how much subtle energy they emitted into the atmosphere and their influence on objects in the surrounding area, which led to its placement in the hierarchy of natural forces.

These forces were recorded in history as pagan gods, making it easy for the layman to understand them. These forces were also measured by the influence they had on the emotional constitution of animals and humans. Since man possessed an abundance of subtle, or life-force energy, he could use this energy to alter the influence of a powerful force by calling its name (vibrational formulae) and speaking to the energy that

resonated behind the said object, be it animal, plant, or star. Speech is vibration, and how words and letters are put together affect other objects vibrating on a subtle level. The enunciation of the names of these forces matched their vibrational level, and in turn they responded in favor of man. The subtle force that is radiated by all animated life was known as fire, and the atmosphere was considered to be water."

Understanding the Kami from this perspective redefines Japanese spirituality for the Western mind. A Japanese deity that rules over the auto industry is not some pagan god, but a force of influence upon the modern world. The force that is responsible for automotive technology can be called upon once it is given a name. Calling upon this name will allow Japanese automotive engineers access to the same ideas that led to the invention of the automobile. Thus, after entreating the *emotional energy* or *kami* that is behind the engineering, manufacturing, and technology of the automotive industry, they will be given the knowledge to advance such. Within Shinto lies the understanding of how to manage and curb the emotional energy, the ki that radiates from objects, thoughts, and ideas in one's experience, for the personal benefit of all, or that of a village, or the nation at large. This way of thinking was an inherent result of the hunter-gatherer culture of ancient Japan. In pre-historic Japan, it was important for ancient man to have a working relationship with the environment that he lived in. It was due to this relationship with nature that men learned how to detect the emotional energy found in all objects and procure such to the benefit of his people. This "technology" enabled prehistoric man with the ability of curbing disastrous weather conditions, flooding, and etc. Through a loving, reverential relationship with his environment, early man found that the vibration of his words expressed in certain emotional states, the fire, motivated a favorable response from the world around him. In a classic work on the topic of Shinto, by Sokyo Ono entitled, *Shinto: The Kami Way*, the author defines the Kami as follows:

"Among the objects or phenomena designated from ancient times as kami are the qualities of growth, fertility, production; natural phenomena, such as wind and thunder; natural objects, such as the sun, mountains, rivers, trees, and rocks; some animals; and ancestral spirits. In the last-named category are the spirits of the Imperial ancestors, the ancestors of noble families, and in a sense all ancestral spirits. Also regarded as kami are the guardian spirits of the land, occupations, and skills; the spirits of national heroes, men of outstanding deeds and virtues, and those who have contributed to civilization, culture, and human welfare; those who have died for the state or community; and the pitiable dead. Not only spirits superior to man, but even some that are regarded as pitiable and weak have nonetheless been considered to be kami."

After having considered the true meaning of the Kami, Ono's statement can be easily conceptualized, as they all refer to forces of emotional influence. It is with this perspective that we begin to understand Shinto not as a religion, but as the science of life; a science that explains how energy is exchanged between objects existing in the same environment. We also become aware that the rituals conducted in Shinto is a way to curtail these energies to suit ones' needs and strengthen their ancestral line.

Appendix C: Raphael Barrio

In my first score of years, I began the delayed path of becoming a magi. It was first necessary to form and educate myself and in the teachings that illuminate us all, the extension of which surpasses the limits of what is tolerable to a free spirit. Then, with sufficient frustrations and disenchantments already to power the enormous drive required, I entered the mission brimming with energy. It was difficult to reformulate that which had been fixed by a robotic, mechanical, dead mind, a generator of subjects ready to serve and feed with blood the insatiable hunger of the artificial system that runs through us all. When I became an alchemist, now immune to the drain of the system, I could see the unspeakable aspects of it. I pushed forward, I met Messiah. I was a few steps behind him on the road to initiation into the Necronomicon. Then he chose the Elders and I, the Ancients and this breach kept us separate from one another and we went to the edge where we met again. Having crossed the limit, the opposites unite. When the Crow Tablets were published I felt a strong call to this work. I felt the same enthusiasm that had driven me to follow in his footsteps in the Necronomicon, and I didn't have the slightest idea what these Tablets dealt with. Without hesitation, and without too much thought, I became initiated in them. This time he followed one step behind me. We separated again, but this time to work closer than ever before in another dimension. They were intense months and he wielded the pen that recorded existence in the work that the reader has in their power at this moment. The Art of Ninzuwu finally dies here, gentlemen, and with it Messiah and I. However the Art and all its followers will continue our existence as a breeze that has already passed, the relative existence has finally ended.

Rafael Barrio
Buenos Aires, September 26, 2013

The Yi Jing Apocrypha of Genghis Khan

Index of the Hexagrams and Related Terms

ABOUT THE EDITOR

Messiah'el Bey, also known as, Warlock Asylum, currently lives in New York City. He has been a practitioner of Asian and Sumerian mysticism for over 15 years. He is currently working on artistic endeavors and raising a family. He can be reached at his current email: warlockasylum@gmail.com

Made in the USA
San Bernardino, CA
18 April 2015